Fulfillment In Ministry

Fulfillment Is Our Portion and Ministry is the Fruit of it!

Rudi Louw

The Holy Scriptures are just that, HOLY.

Statements enclosed in brackets were inserted into Scripture quotations to add emphasis or to clarify the meaning of what is being said in those scriptures. The integrity of God's Word to man was not compromised in any way. Due care and diligence was cautiously exercised to keep the Word of Truth intact.

Table of Contents

Table of Contents

The Marvel of the Holy Bible

1. Uninterrupted Theme and Inspired Thought

It took *1,500 years* to compile the Holy Bible, involving *more than 40 different authors*. <u>Yet</u> the theme and inspired thought of Scripture continues *uninterrupted* from author to author, from beginning till end.

2. Absence of Mythical Stories

Compare philosophies and theories about creation in the Middle East, Europe, Asia, Africa, and Latin America and you'll find mythical scenarios: gods feuding and cutting up other gods to form the heavens and the earth, etc.

In ancient Greek mythology, the Greeks see Atlas carrying the earth on his shoulders. In India, Hindus believe eight elephants carry the earth on their backs.

But in contrast, Job, the oldest book in the Holy Bible, declares that, *"God suspends the earth on nothing."(Job 26:7)*

5

This was said millennia before Isaac Newton discovered the invisible laws of gravity that delicately balance every planet and sun in its individual circuit.

Contrary to every other ancient attempt to give a creation account, *the Holy Bible pictures the creation of the earth in a very scientific manner.*

For example, in Genesis Chapter One, the continents are lifted from the seas then vegetation is formed and later animal life all reproducing *'according to its own kind'*, **thus recognizing the fixed genetic laws.** In addition, we have the bringing forth of man and woman, *all done by God in a dignified and proper manner, without mythological adornments.*

The balance or remainder of the Holy Bible follow suite.

The narratives are **true historical documents**, *faithfully reflecting society and culture* **as history and archaeology would discover them thousands of years later. Not only is the Holy Bible historically accurate, it is also reliable when it deals with scientifically proven subjects.** It was never intended to be a textbook on history, science, mathematics, or medicine. *However, when its writers touch on these subjects,* **they often state facts that scientific advancement would not reveal, or even consider, until thousands of years later.**

While many have doubted the accuracy of the Holy Bible, time and continued research have consistently demonstrated that the Word of God is better informed than its critics.

3. Intactness

Of all the ancient works of substantial size, *the Holy Bible survives intact, against all odds and expectations.*

Compared with other ancient writings, the Holy Bible has more manuscripts as evidence to support it than any ten pieces of classical literature combined!

The plays of William Shakespeare, for instance, were written about four hundred years ago, after the invention of the printing press. Many of his original writings and words have been lost in numerous sections, *yet the Holy Bible's uncanny preservation has weathered thousands of years of wars, contradictions, persecutions, fires and invasions.*

Through the centuries Jewish scribes have preserved the Holy Bible's Old Covenant text, **such as no other manuscripts have ever been preserved. They kept tabs on every letter, syllable, word and paragraph.** *They continued from generation to generation to appoint and train special groups of men within their culture* **whose sole duty it was to** *preserve and transmit these documents <u>with perfect accuracy and fidelity</u>.*

Who ever bothered to count the letters, syllables, or words of Plato, Aristotle, or Seneca for that matter?

When it comes to the New Testament, the actual number of preserved manuscripts is so great that it becomes overwhelming. *There are more than 5,680 Greek manuscripts, more than 10,000 Latin Vulgate manuscripts and at least 9,300 other versions. Further still, there exists an additional 25,000 manuscript copies of portions of the New Testament.* **No other document of antiquity even begins to approach such numbers.**

The closest in comparison is Homer's <u>Iliad</u>, with only 643 manuscripts. The first complete work of Homer only dates back to the 13th century.

4. Unmatched Accuracy in Predictive Foretelling

The Holy Bible is unmatched in accuracy in predictive foretelling. No other ancient work succeeds in this, or even begins to attempt this.

Other books such as the Koran, the Book of Mormon, and parts of the Veda claim divine inspiration; *but none of these books contain predictive foretelling.*

This one undeniable fact we know for certain: *While microscopic scrutiny would show up the imperfections, blemishes, and defects of any work of Man, <u>it magnifies the beauties and perfection of God</u>. Just as every flower displays in accurate detail the reflection and perfection of beauty, <u>so does the Word of Truth when it is scrutinized</u>.*

Historian Philip Schaff wrote:

"Without money and weapons, Jesus the Christ conquered more millions than Alexander, Caesar, Mohammad, and Napoleon. Without science and learning, He (Jesus the Christ) shed more light on things human and divine than all philosophers and scholars combined. Without the eloquence of schools, He (Jesus the Christ) spoke such words of life as was never spoken before or since and produced effects which lie beyond the reach of orator or poet. Without writing a single line, He (Jesus the Christ) set more pens in motion and furnished themes for more sermons, orations, discussions, learned volumes, works of art, and songs of praise **than the whole army of great men of ancient and modern times combined.***"* (*The Person of Christ*, p33. 1913)

Today, there are literally billions of Bibles in more than 2,000 languages.

Isn't it about time you find out what it really has to say?

Hey listen, the Holy Bible is all about Jesus, the Messiah, the Christ...

...and everything about Jesus Christ is really about YOU!!

Study Tips:

Read 2 Corinthians 5:14, 16, 18, 19, and 21.

In the light of these Scriptures, it should be obvious that, if you want to study the Holy Bible, *you should study it in the light of Mankind's redemption!*

Feed daily on **redemption realities** found in the book of Acts, in Romans Chapters One through Eight, and in Ephesians, Colossians, and Galatians, also in 1 Peter Chapter One, 2 Peter Chapter One, James Chapter One, as well as in 1 and 2 Corinthians.

Acknowledgments

I want to acknowledge and thank one of my mentors in the faith, Francois du Toit, for blessing and impacting me with revelation knowledge.

I borrowed the portion on *"The Marvel of the Holy Bible"* from his website: http://www.MirrorWord.net, as students so often feel they have a right to do with things that come from teachers they respect. Just as Galatians 6:6 says, *"Let him who is taught the Word **share in all good things** with him who teaches."*

To all our dear friends and family, for all the love and support, and to all those who helped me with this project:

THANK YOU!

Also, especially to my wife, Carmen;

For keeping me genuine by being my companion in life and partner in ministry,

I love and appreciate you so very much!

Foreword

Thank you for taking the time to read this book.

Let me start off by saying that *I am totally addicted to my Daddy's love for me.*

I am in love with Jesus Christ, *and that is enough for me!*

The love of God is so much more than a doctrine, a philosophy, or a theory. It is so much more and goes so much deeper than knowledge; it way surpasses knowledge.

We are talking heart language here.

I write *to impact people's hearts,* to make them see the mysteries that have been hidden in Father God's heart concerning Christ Jesus, and actually *concerning THEM,* so as to arrest their conscience with it, *that I may introduce them to their original design and to their true selves,* **and present them to themselves perfect in Christ Jesus** *and set them apart unto Him **in love**,* as a chaste virgin.

We are involved with the biggest romance of the ages!

Therefore this book cannot be read as you would a novel: *casually.* It is not a cleverly devised little myth or fable. **It contains** revelation into some things you may or may not have considered before.

It is the TRUTH of God, ultimate TRUTH, and therefore has direct bearing upon YOUR life. **The Word and the Spirit are my witness** *to the reality of these things!*

Be like the people of Berea whom the apostle Paul ministered to in Acts 17:11. Open yourself up to study the revelation contained in this book **to discover for yourself the reality of these things**.

Be forewarned! Do not become guilty of the sins of the Pharisees, **or you too will miss out on the depth of fulfillment God Himself, who is LOVE, wants to give <u>YOU</u>.**

Jesus said of the Pharisees and Sadducees that they strain out every little gnat BUT swallow whole camels. What He meant by that is that *some people seem to have it all together when it comes to doctrine and they love to argue.*

It makes them feel important, but it is nothing other than EMPTY religious and intellectual pride.

They know the Scriptures in and out, and YET they are still so IGNORANT about **REAL TRUTH that is only found in LOVE.**

They are still so ignorant and indifferent **towards the things that REALLY MATTER.**

They are always arguing over the use of *every little jot and tittle* and over the meaning and interpretation of *every word of Scripture.*

The exact thing they accuse everyone else of doing though, the precise thing they judge everyone else for, *they are actually doing themselves.* That is **they often downright misinterpret and twist what is being said,** ***making a big deal of insignificant things, while obscuring or weakening God's real truth: the truth of His LOVE.***

*They are always majoring on minors **because they do not understand the heart of God** **and therefore they constantly miss the whole point of the message**.*

Paul himself said it so beautifully,

*"...the letter kills but **the Spirit BRINGS LIFE;"***

*"...knowledge puffs up, but **LOVE EDIFIES**."*

I say again:

Allow yourself to get caught up in the revelation I am about to share.

Open yourself up to study the insight contained in this book, *not only with a desire to gain knowledge, but also with anticipation **to hear from Father God yourself, to encounter Him through His Word, and to embrace truth, in order to know and believe the LOVE God has for you**, so that you may get so caught up* *in it,* **that you too may receive from Him LOVES' impartation of LIFE.**

This revelation contains within it the voice and call of LOVE Himself to every human being on the face of this earth. *If you take heed to it, and yield yourself fully to it,* **it is custom designed and guaranteed to forever alter and enrich your life!**

"Now I rejoice in the Lord greatly, that now at length you have revived your concern for me. You were indeed concerned for me, but you had no opportunity"

"...Not that I complain of want, **for I have learned the secret that whatever state I am in, to be content.**"

"I know how to be abased, and I know how to abound; **in any** and all circumstances I have learned the secret of facing plenty and facing hunger, abundance and want, **and yet to remain content.** I can do all things in Him who strengthens me."

-Philippians 4:3-19

Prayer

Father we thank you for the ministry of Your precious Holy Spirit.

We thank you for the way He takes us deeper and deeper into the truth of the gospel; into the truth of the Logos revealed.

We thank you Father that the truth that is revealed to us becomes the fuel of our enthusiasm.

We thank you that it becomes the fuel and the energy and the fire; the very passion of our lives.

We thank you Father for what you are teaching us now in the fullness of time, as we sit at your feet.

We thank you for what You have invested in us! We thank you for what You are awakening in us through Your truth!

Father and we realize that that which You have placed within us, and that truth you are sharing with us: **Your revelation of Yourself and of us,** *is more important to us than anything we know!*

Thank you for that eternal incorruptible seed that abides within us!

Thank you for that incorruptible seed of your truth that gets imparted to us and produces a harvest!

Thank you Father that it produces a harvest that will not disappoint Your purpose!

And Father as I am writing here and as others are reading this, as we sit together in Your presence, we thank you for the reality of the hovering of Your Holy Spirit over our hearts and upon the deep within us.

We thank you that as we hear and share together in Your truth and in Your words, it will be more than just the mere words of Man, but it will be *Your* thoughts and intentions that strike us; that cut us to the heart *as deep connects with deep!*

We thank you that the Spirit Himself will engrave upon us; upon our hearts, and that the life we already partake of will be so quickened within us that it will leap up within our inner man; *within our innermost being!*

We thank you God that rivers of living water in potential resides within each and every one of us! And so we thank you that there is and will continue to be an increase also, a gushing forth from our lives; a gushing forth of love and truth and spirit life!

We thank you that it will drastically and radically and effectively touch and transform the nations!

Thank you that it will not be limited to mere words in this book, to a mere few hours' worth of reading, or to even a wonderful set apart time in the secret place with You, but it will indeed so impact our hearts and lives that it will reach for and touch the utter most parts of the earth!

Father that is my expectancy in You as I write this book here in Your presence!

Father, that is indeed my expectation as You awaken my readers and I afresh in our spirits *unto righteousness.*

Father, awaken our hearts and our minds as the truth of Your gospel and of Your word penetrates.

Thank you Jesus!

We worship You!

Amen

Chapter 1

Maintain A Pure Heart!

Paul writes in 1 Thessalonians 5:24 and he says that,

"He who called you is faithful..."

It is so wonderful to discover and to know that God doesn't look at you and see in you potential failure in ministry. God sees in each and every one of us potential success in ministry, and He measures that success by the success of His own achievement on our behalf, in Christ Jesus, *when He both revealed and restored Man's original design and true identity.* And now His commission for us when it comes to ministry *is in the light of what He has already invested in us and in humanity.*

That commission has nothing to do with your sin, it has nothing to do with how many times you have failed in your past. It has nothing to do with how many times you have disappointed whoever expected much of you. Because you see, God commissions you *in terms of His eternal investment in you. He doesn't base His commission on any other qualifying factors.*

God desires every minister of His to live in absolute fulfillment of ministry. *He wants us to taste and see first-hand that God is good. He wants us to have much more evidence of His goodness in our lives and ministry* than just a vague hope for tomorrow; a vague hope for the distant future. *He wants us to personally enjoy the abundant evidence of things not seen, the actual substance. He wants the reality of it burning in our hearts.*

Praise God for the prophets' ministry under the Old Covenant. But we are no longer living in those days! I mean, they saw things that they never tasted of themselves but they saw it prophetically in a distance, *as relating to our day.* We are living in a time now, in the very hour, *when **God wants us to taste and partake of the fullness of the harvest,** amen.* I really believe that.

Listen; God doesn't want us to keep thinking with an Old Covenant prophetic mentality, *looking away from the now* to some unknown distant future and saying that the harvest is not for now, *that there is still four more months and then comes the harvest.* No! He wants us to take off the blinders and to lift up our eyes, to open them wide, and to see that **the fields are already white unto harvest,** meaning that the harvest *is indeed **our portion,*** and not the privilege of the next generation after us, or yet some future, unknown generation. The fullness of the harvest Jesus labored for ***is** our inheritance.* Not our future inheritance, amen; *our inheritance **now!***

I say again: **What Jesus labored for we can enjoy in the now!**

God wants us to taste **the fullness** of that harvest Jesus labored for. *He wants us to be* ***totally fulfilled*** *in our lives and ministry.*

Let's begin by going to 1 Corinthians 9:7.

"Who serves as a soldier at his own expense?"

I am suddenly reminded of what Paul said to Timothy about being a good soldier for Jesus Christ, *about being a good soldier in ministry.*

Paul said in 2 Timothy 2:1-7,

"You then, my son Timothy, ***be strengthened by the grace that is revealed and available in Christ Jesus.****"*

*"****What you have heard from me*** *in the presence of many witnesses,* ***entrust to faithful men*** *(who are they? Those)* ***who will be able to teach others these same things also.****"*

"Endure hardship with us your fellow ministers, as a good soldier of Christ Jesus."

"Remember this: No soldier gets ***entangled*** *in civilian pursuits,* ***since his aim now is to please the one who enlisted him.****"*

"Also, an athlete is not crowned (doesn't taste success), *unless he earnestly competes first, according to the rules, and win."*

*"Take encouragement from this thought: It is the hard-working farmer **who ought to have the first share** of the crops."*

*"Think over what I have said, **for the Lord himself will give you understanding** into everything I am saying."*

But let's get back to the questions Paul asks in 1 Corinthians 9:7. He asks,

"Who serves as a soldier at his own expense?"

"Who plants a vineyard without eating any of its fruit?"

"Who tends a flock without getting some of the milk?"

When it comes to ministry, whose soldier are you? In whose vineyards are you laboring? *The Lord's, amen.* He is the Father of the vineyard according to John 15 and elsewhere in Scripture. And whose flock are we tending? *We are employed by God Himself.* Hallelujah! Can you see that with me?

The One who called us is faithful. He is good to the Nth degree. His reward is with Him, amen!? He is the reward, the maximum reward according to Hebrews 11:6, *the exceedingly great reward* of those who diligently desire to know Him.

They who seek Him for Him and not for what He can do for them; they who passionately seek Him, to know Him, *find Him in Christ!*

Now Paul basically says the same thing there in 1 Corinthians 1:9. He talks about our right in ministry, *our enjoyment in ministry.* It is so important for us not to become so labor conscious *that we totally miss out on the enjoyment that is our portion in ministry.*

And I am not talking about greed now, alright. I am not talking about wringing your hands and seeing dollar signs whenever you think of ministry. You know, *the fringe benefits.* Do you still remember how at one time Jesus' disciples were quarreling with one another over assumed positions of authority that they wanted at Jesus' right hand and at His left? *In their greed they were seeing prestige and honor, fame and fortune, and all the benefits that come with it. Lots and lots and lots of benefits, lots of gold, and lots of benefits.* Jesus was very clear in His response to them in almost every one of the gospels (Matthew 20:25, Mark 10:42 and Luke 22:25-26).

He said to them in Luke 22:25-26,

"The kings of the gentiles exercise lordship over them; and those in authority over them ***are called benefactors.*** ***But not so with you*****;"**

27

*"...**rather let the greatest among you become as the youngest**, and the leader **as a love-slave**; as one who serves."*

1 Corinthians 9:7,

"Who serves as a soldier at his own expense?"

"Who plants a vineyard without eating any of its fruit?"

"Who tends a flock without getting some of the milk?"

Paul is talking about our reward **in Him;** *about enjoying our inheritance in Him.* **He is our inheritance to enjoy!**

Listen, *never become so labor conscious or so reward conscious* that you miss out on the enjoyment of that inheritance in Christ that is our portion in ministry. I am telling you, your labor in ministry can become such a snare, and it has for so many. Paul warned Timothy against this kind of *works and reward consciousness* in 1 Timothy 6:5-12,

*"...men of corrupt minds resist the truth, **supposing that gain is equal to godliness.** From such withdraw yourself."*

"But drawing contentment from godliness is great gain."

"For we brought nothing into this world, and it is certain we can carry nothing out."

28

"And having food and clothing, let us be therewith content."

"But those who desire to be rich fall into temptation and a snare, and into many foolish and harmful lusts, which drown men in destruction and perdition."

*"For the love of money is the root of all evil; and while some have coveted after it, **they have veered off from the faith, and pierced themselves through with many sorrows.***

"But you, O man of God, flee these things, and follow after righteousness, godliness, faith, love, patience and meekness."

*"Fight the good fight of faith; **lay hold of eternal life, where unto you are called,** and have also continually professed that same good confession before many witnesses."*

Eternal life is enjoying your relationship with God, as Daddy. It is you and your best friend Jesus enjoying life together. Eternal life is all about enjoying intimate fellowship with God in the Spirit, amen.

But now before you get all worried and think that God is calling you into deep poverty and self-sacrifice for the sake of the ministry, let's continue to read on there in 1 Corinthians 9, *because neither God nor Jesus is calling you into poverty.* **God calls us to take our eyes off of men and to trust Him instead *because He is faithful!*** He has promised to never leave us nor forsake us, and He has promised to take care of us. *Are we not of more worth to Him than many birds, amen!?*

God is neither unrighteous nor unfaithful; *"**God who called us is faithful!**"* (1 Thessalonians 5:24 & 1 Corinthians 1:9)

Chapter 2

A Larger Definition Of Life!

1 Corinthians 9:7, *"Who serves as a soldier at his own expense?"*

"Who plants a vineyard without eating any of its fruit?"

"Who tends a flock without getting some of the milk?"

We are employed by God **to be partakers** *of the harvest Jesus labored for* and then to minister *out of that fullness!*

Hallelujah!

Now Paul continues in 1 Corinthians 9:8,

"Do I say this on human authority? Does not the Law say the same?"

"For it is written in the Law of Moses, 'You shall not muzzle an ox when it is treading out the grain.' Does God care more about oxen than us?"

Whose grain are we treading out? With whose harvest are we busy with? **God's harvest,** amen, and *"**God who called us is faithful!**"*

Praise God for His grain, **the grain of heaven** *we are fed with and sustained by!*

"I will feed you with the finest of wheat and with honey from the rock!" – Psalm 81:16

"Come and buy honey and milk, come and buy the wine, without money and without price!"
                                                    – Isaiah 55:1

1 Corinthians 1:9 &10,

"Is it for oxen that God is concerned? **Does He not speak entirely for our sake?***"*

*"**It was written for our sake,** because the plowmen should plow in hope and the thresher threshes in hope of **a share in the crop***."*

It was a parable that was used and it's *a parallel that absolutely had us in mind.* Now, our benefits are not all spiritual either, no matter how full our joy is, amen. We do not look to men, we do not look to people, *we look to God as our source and our supply.* **But God still uses people to bless us,** just like Jesus talked about. He said in Matthew 10:8,

"Freely you have received, freely give."

But then He adds in Luke 6:38,

*"…give, and it will be given unto you; good measure, pressed down, shaken together, and running over, **will be put into your lap***."*

Another translation says,

*"Give, and it shall be given unto you: Good measure, pressed down, and shaken together, and running over, **shall men give into your bosom.**"*

Paul continues to say here in 1 Corinthians 9:11-12,

"If we have sown spiritual good among you, is it too much if we reap your material benefits?"

"If others share this rightful claim upon you, do not we still more?"

"Nevertheless, we have not made use of this right, but we endure anything rather than put an obstacle in the way of the gospel of Christ."

Can you see Paul's heart in this scripture? He had a right, a specific claim to these people's material and financial support. But he says that for the sake of the gospel, **for the sake of not putting an obstacle in the way of the gospel, of not causing any reason for offense lest he give people an excuse not to embrace the gospel *fully,*** he did not make use of that right, that legitimate claim.

Now does that mean that Paul is being dumb and stupid, or a little religious, a little over-zealous, or super-spiritual perhaps? Does that mean that now Paul is robbing himself here, and that, shame, poor Paul is now going to have to suffer for it, because He is just too religious and impractical?

No, listen: Paul realizes in whose vineyard he is employed! He realizes just whose flock he is keeping! He realizes just who exactly has enlisted him as a soldier! He realizes just on whose side of this war he is fighting! *He fully grasps and understands that **He who called him is faithful!***

Praise God! Hallelujah!

And so Paul, and really the Holy Spirit, God Himself, in writing about these things wants us to comprehend and understand this as *a principle that actually **works**.*

It is a principle that ***goes beyond*** *what the Law could ever achieve.* It actually works outside of the Law and ***it is much more effective!*** This principle, therefore, has a greater promise attached to it, *a greater blessing than what the Law can promise or produce!* I want you to see it clearly here in this scripture.

Paul states in 1 Corinthians 9:8 how the Law of Moses says, *'An ox is not muzzled while it is treading out the grain.'* Therefore, according to the Law, you have a legal claim; you have a legal right *to **expect** some milk from the flock that you are tending.*

But hallelujah, **a greater than Moses has come!**

34

We are no longer dealing with principles according to the Law. **The Law has been done away with in Christ.**

We are now dealing with what has been revealed and made known in Christ.

We are dealing with greater realities, better promises.

We are dealing with more powerful and more effective principles; *greater principles!*

Paul says that, *'according to the Law, you have a legal claim, a legal right to **expect** some milk from the flock that you are tending.'* *'**But,**'* he says, *'I want to teach and reveal to you **a greater principle of support** which is larger than the Law and its definition. It's much bigger than the Law's system of support! It's not as limited! It's bigger than the Law, amen! It's a larger measure!'*

Hallelujah!

That excites me, because I have seen in my life many ministries *crippled* because their whole financial budget mentality has been restricted and limited by the Law and to the Law. And that Law says, *'Pay your tithes; **otherwise the Levites won't make it!**'* Listen; a Law-mentality will restrict you every time! A lack-conscious financial budget, a lack-conscious mentality will restrict you every time!

The Law measures in terms of lack; *it is always lack conscious.*

But, in contrast, grace always measures in terms of abundance, in terms of God's abundance towards me, *in terms of the abundance of His provision already made available to me in Christ.*

The Law says, *'You cannot muzzle an ox while it is treading out the grain'*

So brethren, here we are, and we are still trying to live by the Law. And it is right; there is nothing wrong with it on the surface. The Law gives its applause to your decision. **But in Christ there is a higher way!**

There is a higher way which *the New Testament* **Scriptures teach us.**

There is a place of **living in <u>God's</u> provision** that God has in mind for His people.

If we can just discover whose soldier we are, in whose vineyard we work, whose flock we tend, we would realize that **we are not looking to the vineyard or the flock to sustain our needs,** *but we're looking totally to our heavenly Father who knows we have need of these things!*

I mean if we can merely grasp whose kids we are, if we can understand, if we can fully comprehend *whom it is that has **committed Himself to taking care of us and** simply know* and believe the love **our Daddy has _for us_**, we will be set free in our inner-man to put our trust _fully_ in Him.

Amen!

Hallelujah!

So it is quite alright to agree with the law to no longer muzzle the ox while it is treading out the grain. I am not knocking those who still believe in the Law and who still live by the Law. Praise God for the Law's contribution.

But Paul made a discovery in his ministry; _he discovered a better and larger definition of life and ministry than the limited definition of it under the Law._

Paul made that discovery _when he discovered the constraining power of the gospel, the truth of it, the very faith of God, and_ **the intensity of that love and joy produced by it in his spirit.**

He realized that the gospel had taken the limits off. The love of God found in the gospel had removed all restrictions.

That large, large measure of the love of God in the gospel now constraining him was out of all proportions to the constraints of the Law.

He suddenly found himself no longer under the constraints of thinking and trying to work out and calculate, *'Well, if I go to that place, will they be able to support me there?'* Or thinking and calculating, *'If I go here, or say I go there, will there be enough? I mean, which decision will bring in the most…?'* And so you then limit your strategy to the Law, to a natural reward system, to whether there is enough grain to gain!

But listen, Paul now sees his strategy in the light of God's rich deposit, *in the light of God's richness in his spirit.* And he suddenly now, perhaps even surprisingly so, finds himself under a new kind of obligation, a new kind of necessity, a new kind of constraining force, a new kind of motivation deposited in his spirit, a compelling inspiration and undying love that comes from his heart, *imparted to him and activated within him by a revelation of the love of God.*

You see, this was not a religious obligation, a legalistic motivation, but a motivation *deposited within his spirit.* **It was an inspiration from the heart. It was love's compelling!**

A pastor friend of mine asked me the other day, *'What do you guys teach about giving at your church? Do you teach tithing at all?'*

When I replied that we did not, he had a very perplexed look upon his face and asked, *'Then how in the world can you afford to do all the things you are doing?'*

This guy is very big on tithing. In fact, if you are a part of their fellowship, they will show up at your home to confront you and make you feel all guilty and ashamed if you, for whatever reason, were unable to pay your tithe in the past two weeks.

The Scriptures teach us something different in the New Covenant *because God trusts in the work of the gospel in our hearts.* He trusts in the work of redemption realities, *in the working of His Spirit of Truth making plain and emphasizing those redemption realities in your spirit.*

Listen; the Holy Spirit, through Paul, teaches us not to give in reluctance *as if compelled and manipulated to do so under compulsion and obligation.*

Can you see how Law-mindedness, or a legalistic mentality as a motivation, *can only produce reluctance?* **It has reluctance as a result.** This is the fruit of remaining under the compulsion of the Law.

But what kind of obedience is God looking for, what is God looking for? **God is looking for a heart,** *immersed in the truth of His love and inspired by that love.*

I say again: *He is looking for a heart immersed in love, and inspired by love!*

God is looking for a heart that cries out and knows and rests secure in the fact that, *'God, You are my portion in life!'*

My portion in life has got nothing to do with how large a bank account I am holding onto; with how large a barn I am planning to build, but *'You are my portion in life, Oh Lord!'*

God wants us to discover, along with Paul, the absoluteness, the contentment, the absolute fulfillment of living in His provision, *living in the fullness of Christ's provision,* **so that He becomes my total sufficiency.**

Chapter 3

The Lord Is My Portion!

We will get back to 1 Corinthians 9, but let's just quickly take a look at Psalm 16 and see what David wrote there.

Psalm 16:5,

"The Lord is my chosen portion, and my cup."

And so we think, *'Shame man, poor fellows, let's feel sorry for them. These guys, they just have the Lord as their portion and nothing else. They live on barely-get-along street, next to grumble-alley!'*

I mean the rest of the tribes of Israel, if you were to go back and study it, you would find how the tribes were each allotted their portion of land, but the Levites only had the Lord as their portion.

'Shame, the poor Levites, you know, they are going to just have to learn to live off of the crumbs that fall off of the table, because they only have the Lord as their portion.'

No man, nonsense!

Here is David, and he is the king, *and he lacks in nothing, amen,* and even though he is of the tribe of Judah, *he sees himself as a Levite.*

The word **Levite** in the Hebrew means *a joined one.*

It is interesting to note that the Levites were the sons of Zadok, and **Tzadok** in the Hebrew means *righteousness.* In other words, **the Levites were the joined ones through righteousness.**

Hallelujah!

Now, because David, being a king, set apart by God, *understood righteousness, he understood what it was to be so intimately linked up with God,* therefore he saw himself as a Levite, and began to declare, *"The Lord is my portion and my cup!"*

Do you remember what David said in Psalm 23 about his cup? He said, *"My cup runs over!"*

Now that's a large portion of "Lord" he had, amen! Ha... ha... ha...

Psalm 16:5 & 6,

"The Lord is my portion and my cup; You hold my lot in Your hands! The boundary lines have fallen for me in pleasant places; surely, I have a delightful inheritance!"

42

We can go and just kind of lend an ear to how the other guys in the other tribes are measuring, you know, *what they have received.*

'Oh, you know I wish I had that kind of tree in my garden, but O well, you know, the lot is always too small, not quite big enough, or not inclusive enough. Now if I could just include that river down there, or if I could just have that mountain, or this or that… But, you know, it's normal I guess, everybody is always just a little bit disappointed. It's just our lot in life, man, isn't it? I mean, It's quite normal to feel just a little bit disappointed ...isn't it!?'

Because he always knows back in his mind that, *'There is more to life than what I have measured out to me!'*

And so you see, people always feel desperately responsible, you know, to justify their being on this planet. So it is just natural to feel that, you know, *'the larger my bank account, the larger the portion of land that I can possess, the more confident I would be as an individual, living and breathing and surviving on this planet. I mean, after all, I have to justify my existence, you see!'*

But listen, **when you discover His justification of you, the righteousness He has given you, the righteousness He has designed you in and brought you forth in and fully restored you to, then you taste of** a different vine, you eat of a different loaf of bread, you drink from a different source, *and a new sense of fulfillment lives in your spirit.*

And you see, **that sense of fulfillment makes you immune to a spirit of competition.** It makes you immune to *always measuring and comparing yourself against others, always feeling left out, always feeling like you don't quite measure up.* You see, that sense of fulfillment *separates you from feelings of, 'Oh, shame, Abraham, you missed out. Just look at Lot, you know, he chose the better portion.'*

But listen, let me tell you something: Lot could choose even the ends of the earth, if he could see that far, he could choose the most beautiful part of the earth, *but it still would not rob Abraham!* **Because you see, Abraham's portion was the Lord!**

God wants us to be totally convinced in our spirits that He, the Lord our God, *is our portion!*

"The lines have fallen for me in pleasant places; surely, I have the best inheritance!!"

The Afrikaans translation says: *"My inheritance is exceptionally beautiful to me!"*

That's what our attitude should be, amen!

David basically says, *"I cannot find any fault with what God has given me; there is no hint of it, none whatsoever!"*

I mean, there was Israel, on their way to the largest natural promise of inheritance ever given to Man, a land flowing with milk and honey and abundance. But they still grumble and moan and groan and complain, and they talk in terms of what their senses could perceive *only in the moment.* All they could *see* was wilderness. They *see* desert, they *see* the sun, **but they could not <u>see</u> the reality of the Lord as their portion!**

But David discovers that he's a Levite, even though in the natural he isn't, but still he discovers that he is a Levite, *that **he is joined to God in covenant relationship.***

He says, Psalm 16:7-8,

*"I bless the Lord who gives me counsel; in the night also my heart instructs me. I keep the Lord always before me; **because He is at my right hand,** I shall not be moved."*

This is the secret to fulfillment: **I keep the Lord always before me!**

Verse 9 says,

"Therefore my heart is glad, and my soul rejoices…"

That word *"soul"* is the word for glory in the Hebrew, the word **kabod,** which means **weight.**

He is talking about the weight of your evaluation of God's deposit in you!

Some translation has it as *"tongue",* but it goes along with that same thought and it speaks of the same thing: *because of that glory inside of your spirit, your tongue has to respond!*

Therefore David says in verse 10,

"My body also dwells secure, for thou dost not give me up to Sheol, or let thy godly one see the Pit."

Hey listen, those two scriptures meant something to Jesus, even in the grave, amen. Those were the only two scriptures Jesus had while going through hell, amen. I mean everything left Him and abandoned Him except for the Word; the *Logos.* It was exactly because of His attachment, as a man, to the word in His spirit, that God could raise Him from the dead. It would have been impossible for Jesus Christ, as a man, to go through with the experience of the cross and keep His eyes on the resurrection, *if it weren't for these two scriptures deposited in His spirit.*

Sometimes we have this wrong idea that somehow when Jesus was born, He was born with some kind of an automatic little computer and He had all the Scriptures deposited already within His spirit and He knew the whole volume of Scripture off by heart, just like that! No man, He had to study and meditate on the Scriptures and come to a place where He personally appreciated and appropriated and chose to believe the *Logos,* the truth of the word, for Himself! And through that He was able to endure the cross and God could raise Him from the dead! While He was hanging there on that cross, and cried out, He began quoting that which was in Him. He began quoting the Scriptures and He started by quoting Psalm 22. *He already saw the undoing of the Fall; the joy set before Him!* He was quoting from the volume of the book because He already knew by the Spirit of Truth, by the Spirit of revelation knowledge, exactly what the prophets spoke concerning Him. He appreciated and appropriated that word. He believed it and He held onto that word for Himself!

Peter spoke of this, how Jesus stood on that promise and was thereby raised. You can go read it there for yourself in Acts 2:24-28. **Jesus knew and believed that His body would not see corruption, neither would His Father ever abandon Him, nor leave His soul in Sheol!**

But I am getting sidetracked now. Let's get back to Psalm 16.

Verse 11 says,

*"Thou dost show me the path of life; in thy presence, there is **fullness of joy!**"*

*"In thy right hand are **pleasures for evermore!**"*

The Afrikaans translation puts it so beautifully, it says,

"Fulfillment, yes, saturation and satisfaction of joy, of pleasure, is being face to face with You!"

That is fulfilled living, amen!

"Fulfillment; fullness of joy!"

It means that **while you are living face to face with Him, fully embraced in His bosom, experiencing His presence, His love, *you realize that you don't need anything extra!*** Because now you are not living on the fringes but, you find your life, *in the very focus of His favor!* **Grasping that you are indeed the apple of His eye!**

"Fullness of joy!"

You really don't need anything extra!

I mean, they can come and bless you with a 100 million dollars but it is not going to get any more joy out of you, *out of your spirit, than what you already enjoy within you; within your innermost being.*

Fullness of joy is measured by your spirit's fulfillment, amen!

There is nothing greater than your spirit's fulfillment! Nothing can be added to that!

Nothing extra could add to that joy!

"Because, the Lord is my portion!"

Hallelujah!

Do you see that David began to touch and tap into some fulfillment that was larger than what the Law permitted him and his people to walk in?!

It was even larger than what the natural senses could provide!

Praise God that we, too, are no longer just oxen, treading out grain, and hoping, you know, for our little share of grain. But your heavenly Father, who feeds the birds, *feeds you and sustains you and is committed to you.*

He is more committed to you than He is to them, just as much as you are more committed to your loved ones, to your little ones, than you are to anything else.

You are of much more value to Him than they, amen.

He sustains your life! He sustains you, amen!

That means He is committed to you!

Listen; He is jealous over you. That means he is protective over you!

He yearns with jealous anticipation for the spirit which He made to dwell within you!

He longs for communion with you!

He longs for your faith in His love! He longs for your absolute trust in Him!

Okay, so, that was David's testimony, but we are now still in 1 Corinthians 9.

Chapter 4

The Old System And Its Rights

Paul said in 1 Corinthians 9:9-12,

"For it is written in the Law of Moses, 'You shall not muzzle an ox when it is treading out the grain'. Is it for oxen that God is concerned? Does He not speak entirely for our sake? It was written for our sake, because the plowman should plow in hope and the thresher thresh in hope of a share in the crop. **If we have sown spiritual good among you, is it too much if we reap your material benefits? If others share this rightful claim upon you, do not we still more?"**

But now he says there in the rest of verse 12,

"Nevertheless, we have not made use of this right, but we endure anything, rather than put an obstacle in the way of the gospel of Christ."

You see, Paul realizes that his commission was to preach the gospel *in such a way* that many would believe. And he also realized that Mankind in their mindset had become so linked to and limited by the financial systems of this world that if there should be any subtle hint even, in his ministry, indicating that he was ministering because he was looking at the size of their pockets, it would cause an obstacle, and then his ministry to them would be in vain and it would fail them.

He knew he had to plant a seed of the word into their spirits. **So he would rather endure, and he would rather not make any mention of his financial rights, or make any claim upon their finances whatsoever. He would place no obstacle, no burden upon their lives** *because he wanted to win them; he wanted to win their hearts and not their money, amen. Do you see that!?*

Listen; God is not interested in their pocketbooks; *He is interested in them,* ***in loving them, in winning their hearts!***

And so Paul realized this, and started ministering from that perspective *and from that motivation,* **compelled by the love of Christ alone!**

Love was his *motivation* in ministry. He had no other motivation; no hidden agenda!

That's why he says in verse 13,

"Do you not know that those who are employed in the temple service get their food from the temple, and those who share in the altar, share in the sacrificial offerings?"

Verse 14,

"In the same way, the Lord commanded that those who proclaim the gospel should get their living by the gospel."

I want you to notice that he is basically quoting what Jesus said in Luke 10:1-9 *when He sent out the seventy and told them that they should live by the gospel and **trust God; trusting that God would provide for them.***

Paul says in 1 Corinthians 9:15,

*"**That is why I have made no use of any of these rights,** nor am I writing this to secure any such provision."*

Paul realizes that **faith doesn't work by hints!**

So he says, '*I am not trying to hint, or trying to make provision for the future, for some unforeseen future need perhaps, so that if I end up in a bind somewhere, then you can react and say, 'Shame, you know, poor Paul, he has now really sacrificed all he had for the gospel, so let's just help him out and have pity on him, and help support his struggling ministry.'*

Paul could have easily done that, amen. He could have easily played on people's emotions and relied on their empathy and milked them for all they had.

I mean, even Peter at one time had to have considered these things, because there came a day when he asked a potent question of

Jesus: *'Jesus, you know, what are we going to get for all this? I mean we have forsaken everything for You and for the kingdom, what are we to expect?'*

Do you remember Jesus' response?

Jesus says, Luke 18:29,

*"Not one of you who have given up his home, his wife, brothers, sisters, parents, for My sake and for the kingdom and for the gospel, **will lose anything.** I can guarantee you only this: **You will receive manifold more in this time, yes in this life.** You may have to suffer persecution in this world for your commitment to Me and your strong stand, **but you will receive a hundredfold return in eternal life,** (in the form of abundant life; you will enjoy life more abundantly, not only now, but) **even in the ages to come."***

I mean, Jesus could have answered Peter, *'Well, wonderful, you know, Peter, I commend you guys, you guys have really overextended yourselves in giving up everything you've got, so let Me only assure you merely of this: **One day in heaven, that's when it is all going to be given back to you,** and you can look forward to the day that you are going to have an especially spectacular big mansion in the sky!'*

But No! You see, He didn't say that. *He didn't talk that kind of useless religious nonsense!* Jesus knew that what He had to give,

54

everything that *His is,* and everything that *is His,* all that abundance He has to give, *is ours, in this life, and in the life that is to come!*

Hallelujah!

In other words: '***What you are beginning to enjoy with Me now, in intimate union with the Father, in abundant living, in a life of bliss, enjoying life more fully together with God, that reality of life more abundantly you will continue to enjoy, starting now and continuing for ages yet to come, even for all eternity.'***

Listen; stop limiting your hope to an intangible pie in the sky, to non-existent things that are out there, somewhere in the unknown by and by, **because God has given the fullness of life to us here and now, in this world. Yes, here, even in this world;** a world full of persecutions and trials and tribulations.

I say again: **God has given Himself to us, and in the giving of Himself to us in covenant commitment, He has given fullness of life to us in the here and now, *IN THIS LIFE!***

And so Paul says, *"I even glory in the midst of tribulations!"*

He says, *"Because the tribulations do not have what it takes to cancel God's gift **in me** – my design, my true identity* (or to cancel God's Gift

55

of Himself; to cancel God's commitment to me as His child!)*"

'Therefore I glory in tribulations, because even tribulation itself will be swallowed up by us, it will be swallowed up by the light in us, it will be swallowed up to reflect His glory!'

Amen, so why worry about the tribulations? God has placed enough power in the gospel to rescue me every time! God has placed enough in me, through the gospel, to overcome the tribulations that come my way, and comes against all Men, amen!

John says, *"This is the victory that overcomes this world, **every trail and tribulation**; this is the victory, even **our faith!**"*

Jesus says, *"Be of good cheer! I have overcome the world!"*

He doesn't say, *'All right you guys I am about to leave you now, but I am all nervous now, because, you know, I know you are frail people and you might fail Me, so let Me just prepare you guys by saying, brace yourselves, just hang in there till the bitter end, you know, because you are going to have a hard time living in this world, and you are going to be dirt poor, and you are going to have to suffer, so just try and hang in there till the bitter end!'*

No, He says, *"Be of good cheer, I have overcome this world!"*

So he doesn't immobilize His saints. No, *He mobilizes them and encourages them,* **he cheers them up!**

Do you pick up on the tone of His voice?

He doesn't tell them, *'Oh, you know, you are going to have such a hard time!'*

'No,' He says, *'You might have persecution; you might face various trials and tribulation,* **but be of good cheer,** *I have overcome the world, amen,* **and you are My trophies; you are My treasures! If I care that much for you; if I am for you, then what can prevail against you!***'*

So, Paul says, 1 Corinthians 9:15,

"I have not made use of any of these rights to your finances and your possessions, and I am not writing this to hint towards it either, for I would rather die than have anyone deprive me of my ground for boasting."

He was talking about the fact that His ground for boasting, **his confidence** was in Jesus and in what He has revealed and restored; it was in the cross of Jesus Christ, and what was accomplished there on his behalf, and our behalf, to our benefit.

*His confidence was not in his own strength or in his own abilities and achievements. **His confidence was in God and not in himself.***

He would rather die than have anyone take away this new found confidence, this reliance upon God, *this faith.*

He would rather die than lose sight of faith! He would rather die than lose the faith of God! He would rather die than lose focus! He would rather die than forget God's love and lose trust in God! He would rather die than lose his inheritance. He would rather die than betray his birthright for a bowl of Lentil soup, or any other bowl of lethal soup. **He refused to live by anything less than the abundance that was already his in Christ Jesus!**

Hallelujah!

1 Corinthians 9:16,

"For if I preach the gospel, it gives me no grounds for boasting, for necessity is laid upon me. Woe to me if I do not preach the gospel!"

Do you understand that it is revealed here in this scripture, and many other places, *that there is a new Law that Paul operates under?*

Under the Law of Moses, you cannot muzzle the ox while it's treading out the grain. *But it was only serving as a prophetic picture, pointing to a new Law.*

There is a new Law that is now at work. There is a new Law that is now constraining Paul! It is called: **The Law of Faith!** It is called: **The Law of Love!**

He says, *'I want to take you beyond the Law of Moses!'*

He says, *'I mean, under that old system, let the ox eat all that he can. But I didn't take advantage of that privilege and that right just because it's legal under that old system, just because that is the way that old system functioned.'*

He says, *'No, I agree, let that ox eat all that he can. But let it be under the new system, let it be by the new and living way. Because you see, I am operating under another Law, a new Law, amen. It's the Law of Christ! The Law of trust! It's the Law of love!'*

Hallelujah!

So his preaching of the gospel is not effected by the size of the commission made on the deal. But that necessity for it, that necessity burning in his spirit to preach the gospel, that necessity **inspired by love alone,** *is the only persuasion that compels his heart.*

I want you to know that if this same persuasion becomes the fuel of your spirit, the necessity burning within you, ***you will also always be free from a financial strain upon your ministry!***

So many well-meaning ministries today, even the big ones – especially the big ones – are caught up in the financial systems of this world **because they are still measuring their**

finances by the Law of Moses: *You've got to tithe! And you cannot muzzle the ox!* And so they've got to keep writing their little letters of persuasion and try and get you to give more. And their envelopes are always included and handed out everywhere, and they are always saying, *'Please,'* and even the postage is paid for, *to try and make it easier on you to give,* **and more convenient for them.**

But Paul says, *"God does not love for you to give under compulsion!"* **God doesn't want it to be that way!**

So, unless the impact of ministry, **unless the impact of God's love ministry to you, so compels you to give, yourself, your body, your very being, in ministry to Him, and to others, as a sacrifice <u>alive in Him</u>, then forget about ministry. But don't be moved by any other compulsion!**

Paul says, *"Woe to me if I do not preach the gospel."* And again we think, *'Shame, you know, poor Paul, you know, he is just like the Levites, they only had God as their portion! The rest of the guys, you know, they could really possess the land, and they could have it so good, but the poor Levites…'*

I thank God for David. We have already looked at him, he is our example of that, *"The Lord is my portion; the lines have fallen for me in pleasant places* …**in pleasant places!"**

Listen, if you find that the enemy has come, that the thief comes to limit your joy, immediately get into the presence of God *by setting your mind on things that are above!* Don't allow your mind to wander off into darkness and don't entertain dark thoughts. Immediately get into the presence of God. Set your mind on things that are above! Deliberately renew your mind to the truth of the Scriptures, to the truth of your sonship and His indwelling, to the truth of His nearness and His power available immediately to you in Him!

"Think on these things," Paul says. Remind yourself of the truth of the gospel, *of what you know concerning your true identity, and your Daddy's love for you!* Look away unto Jesus, the author and perfecter of your faith! Awaken unto your righteousness, *for in His presence is fullness of joy!* Amen! Hallelujah! *"There is joy and peace in believing!"* - Romans 15:13.

God guarantees our fulfillment, He guarantees fulfillment in ministry according to the New Covenant.

***He Himself** is the guarantee of our fulfillment, amen!*

Your fulfillment does not depend on how much was given to you in offerings this month. Your fulfillment does not depend on how many people you impressed this month, earning their applause, or earning some kind of reward from them through your good preaching. **Your**

fulfillment is the direct fruit of your dwelling in His presence, of your intimate love-affair, of your fellowship with Him.

In His presence *there is fullness of joy!*

Paul says in 1 Corinthians 9:17,

*"For if I do this **of my own will,** I have a reward…"*

Paul understands that **if it's his own will,** if he kind of talked himself into it and imagined and willed himself into it, and there is some kind of legalistic motivation attached to it, *then he would also justify and persuade himself, or think himself to have a right to the reward of other people's finances and possessions, especially the ones he is ministering to.*

Remember, *if we look at 1 Corinthians 1:26,* how Paul said,

"Consider your call brethren, not many of you were considered to be wise according to worldly standards, not many were physically attractive or powerful and strong in the flesh, not many were of noble birth, or influential, or wealthy; but God chose you none the less!"

He says in verse 9, *"**God has called us into the fellowship of His Son**"*

And here in 1 Corinthians 9, I believe Paul is discussing and revealing **his own**

consideration of his call. He is revealing *his motivation in ministry.*

There was a time in Paul's own life where that was what he was doing in his own spirit. He was considering the motivation of his own heart, he was considering his call, he was asking himself and trying to discover, *'Now why go through all this? I mean, why am I giving myself to this thing called ministry, why am I putting myself through all this? I mean, it has been more than once now that I've landed in prison for this thing called ministry. I've ended up in prison **because of my passion, because of this motivation, this compelling force within me.** I mean, just look at me, I find myself often in odd situations, and in sometimes difficult situations; in various trials and tribulations and contradictions and persecutions…'*

And we can add our five cents and say, *'Yes, Paul, if only your faith was strong enough. If only you could adjust your mentality in ministry, or maybe your modus-operandi. I mean, Paul, you can have it much better in life. You were at one time such a favorite guy under the system, so popular! Why can't you go back to that, why can't you just rejoin the system?'*

And here Paul himself was also considering, *'What am I doing this for? I mean, here I am, I am facing so many dangers all around and everywhere: dangers from robbers and dangers from wild beasts, and dangers in the cities, and dangers even among the country folk, crossing dangerous rivers and seas,* **and yet I keep having this constant driving force on the inside, this compelling motivation within me, inspiring me and compelling me all the time**', and so he considers his call and reveals his motives to these believers whom he is writing to, and to us.

He says in 1 Corinthians 9:17,

*"For if I do this **of my own will,** I have a reward…"*

He says,

"I am not doing this of my own free will, if I did, then I could have a claim like the rest of the ministers I run into everywhere I go, I could have a claim and a demand to a certain portion of your income. I could make my claim upon some consistent support: 'Please sir, would you mind, I need your support! I'll even send you a monthly newsletter and a free return-envelope in the mail! All you have to do is fill in the block and say exactly how much money you are going to give me once a month. We can even make it so it comes out on automatic bank draft, just like clockwork, for your convenience, sir, and for mine, and that way you don't even have to be concerned about it at all, you know. I mean, you wouldn't even have to worry whether you have remembered to give your support or pay your tithe this month, it just all happens so conveniently,

automatically, no emotional involvement required …and no personal connection either."

No man, listen, let me just say this outright, in black and white, right here in this book. And I can personally guarantee you that it is in line with the New Testament, it is the word of God: **While you limit ministry to that legalistic reward mentality, to a job with a paycheck attached to it, you will always wrestle with it emotionally and struggle financially!** I guarantee it, because you are linking yourself up to a coin, you are limiting your life to serving the almighty dollar.

In Mark 12, Jesus said,

*"Show me a coin. Whose inscription is upon that coin? They answered, 'Caesar's,' and then He said, 'Pay to Caesar what belongs to him, **but give to God what is His!**'"*

And even now I can hear the Spirit saying through Jesus, *"**Show me a man. Whose inscription is engraved within that man's spirit, within his being, even within Caesar's being? Give to God what belongs to Him!**"*

Amen! Give to God **what He deserves, what His love for you deserves!** *Give Him your heart and your whole being! It belongs to Him!* Don't go and measure your life by money. Don't go measure your worth by coins! You can weigh and sell birds that way, **but not**

people! You are worth to God so much more than birds! Don't fall into the snare of selling your ministry! **People will put any price upon the anointing. They will be prepared to pay any price for it, *but you are not for sale!***

When the women broke that expensive alabaster box, she did not consider it. She refused to calculate the years' worth of wages, the year's labor that bought that precious ointment! *It was her joy to pour it out on Jesus' feet!*

I remind you that it was Judas who sat there *and went shipwreck in his soul because he counted and calculated **and measured and weighed himself right out of his inheritance!***

He sat there and smelled the precious perfume, that costly perfume, and said to himself, *'This adoration, this appreciation, this measure of worth is too good to be true. This kingdom thing, this gospel, this Jesus isn't worth all that!'*

'I mean, how can this woman even consider wasting that costly perfume like this? Hasn't she given any consideration to her own well-being, to her own status in life, to her future even? If she had she would have realized that she cannot afford to do this. Life is difficult enough as it is. That money, that precious resource could have been better spent in other ways! She should have given it to me instead

of wasting it like this. I would have done a better job managing that money and spending it more wisely!'

Listen; don't let Judas dictate to you what you do with your life! Don't allow Judas to try and box you in again! Don't let any Judas put a for sale sign on you! **Don't sell yourself short, your life is making a much bigger impact than you even realize or can possibly know.** *Just continue to let the fullness of the fragrance of your life promote the knowledge of God's grace!*

I mean, if Jesus couldn't set us that free, so that we can be truly free, even from the world's systems, *then we've got a poor redemption.*

It sounds so irresponsible when Jesus says, *'Don't be anxious about your life!'* But He says, *'Hey, listen, **your heavenly Father knows that you have need of all these things!** Come on man, do you see any anxious birds flying around, saying to themselves, 'O, how are we going to get everything together today to feed ourselves, you know, we only have a couple of hours left, and we still have to feed our little babies?!'*

'And so those birds are suddenly so caught up in a mentality of 'I've got to survive!'

'Ha... ha... ha... No! Birds don't do that!'

'Why not?'

'Because there is no need for them to do so!
**Your heavenly Father feeds them! And
listen, you are not in a survival game either!
Are you not of much more value to your
heavenly Father than they?'**

Hallelujah!

We are not just trapped in a survival game, like
the world wants us to believe, amen.

**We are more than conquerors through Him
who loves us!**

So often we read these ministry newsletters
people send out and we think, *'Wow, shame, if
I don't support this person in what they are
trying to do, they are going to fail, and their
ministry is going to fall apart.'*

Ha… ha… ha…

**No! Listen; when Jesus commissions us,
He knows what He has in us in terms of His
investment in us and in terms of His
deposit in us. And if that deposit is the true
gospel only, and not some fringe benefit
mentality, then that gospel will sustain your
life and your ministry, and you'll discover
that even in your gray hair years, God
sustains your life!**

You will be able to say to others and have this
testimony that *God has sustained you
throughout your life and that you never had a
dull moment,* amen!

I tell you, that was Paul's secret, and the secret from which he writes here in 1 Corinthians 9:17.

If Paul was living by that fringe benefit mentality, that legalistic reward mentality, that job and paycheck mentality, then surely he would have had the right to lay claim upon their support, and he could have justified it and said that he could legally do it. But instead he said, *"I did not make use of it!"* **He stressed that he did not want to present an obstacle to the gospel. The gospel's reception, the gospel itself, what it promises *and deliver* was more precious than their support.**

1 Corinthians 9:17,

"For if I do this of my own will then I have a reward, but if not of my own will, I am entrusted with a commission,"

Hallelujah!

God has faith in you!

Isn't that wonderful!?

God has faith in me!

And as long as He has faith in me, *as long as His love and trust inspires me, as long as that love compels me, I'm entrusted with a pure heart, with pure motives.* And I am *thereby also entrusted with a commission,* **and ministry flows from that, it flows from that!**

His love commissions me and that commission tells me that He has faith in me!

Hallelujah!

Now in verse 18 Paul asks the question, and this is his conclusion. This is Paul's conclusion after his consideration of the call to be a minister of the New Covenant.

He asks: *"What then is my reward?"*

Chapter 5

What Is Your True Reward?

1 Corinthians 9:18,

"What then is my reward?"

I mean, we can read that and think, *'Yes, Paul, what's in this for me, what's in this? What's my reward? Maybe if I really go for it, and I apply myself, then maybe one day I, too, can drive a BMW or a very nice Mercedes Benz or some other sports car or luxury vehicle, depending on my preference. And I'll be living in that fantastic mansion; you know, the one in the gated community with a pool and what have you, or whatever, and I'll have all these nice things. So Praise God, you know, I'm going to give it all I've got!'*

But listen man, if the BMW or a fat bank account is your reward you're working for, woe to you! Listen; that metal box is merely a vehicle. It's a practical means of getting from point A to point B. The thing that really counts is not the vehicle you drive, but it is Ephesians 6: *"The shoes; the preparation within you, within your heart, for the mobilization of the gospel through you, into the ears and hearts of your friends and neighbors, and strangers even, going all the way around the globe, even*

*going into and reaching to the remote places;
to the very ends of the earth."*

If you allow the truth of the gospel to do a work
in your heart, and you make that preparation
within your heart of the full embrace of the
gospel your focus, your desire, and the passion
and motivation of your spirit, *you will soon
discover that God will give you everything
needed for life and ministry.*

He will supply the wheels and wings and shoes
and planes and ships and housing, *and
whatever you need to carry and convey and
share the truth of the gospel, the truth of His
love, amen!*

And let me tell you now, God will bless you
with the best that's available. You don't have
to live with a poverty mindset either, settling for
unreliable transport or whatever. God's not
limited to a donkey, amen!

But let me also tell you that many who have
swallowed the whole prosperity message have
gotten so twisted in their whole faith mentality
that they think that the stuff they are *"believing
for," '...Oh, it's there for us brother, to enrich
the soul.'* No, listen; your soul cannot eat that
stuff, precious one. It's empty; there is no real
satisfaction in any of it! *"Life is more than food
and clothing! Man shall not live by bread
alone, but by that sustaining gospel that
proceeds from the mouth of God!"* (Matthew
6:25, Luke 12:23, Matthew 4:4)

If your fulfillment is not *drinking from the fountain,* I mean, if your fulfillment in life is the salary at the end of the month or whatever nice thing you can kind of see as your reward, *then you still do not understand what **fulfillment** is all about.* You do not understand what **eternal life, life more abundantly in Him,** is all about!

Listen don't be cheated, don't settle for anything less than what God calls fulfillment! Don't allow yourself to be cheated by things that fade and see that as your reward. No man! Hey listen; **you have an unfading reward, an unfading treasure in your spirit. And it's yours because the lines have fallen for you in pleasant places, in satisfying places, in places of fulfillment!**

God has said, *"You are My portion!"* and I have said to Him, *"You are my portion!"*

We are His Levites, joined together with Him in the Spirit; knitted together!

We are joined at the hip, linked in the heart! There is no separation between us!

We are wrapped up in a love affair with our God, with Him who is love! He is the lover of our souls!

We are His inheritance, and He is ours! We are His legal portion! We are God's inheritance!

You can go read it for yourself there in Ephesians 1:18. We are His legal portion. It literally says in the Greek: **we are God's inheritance!**

Hallelujah!

You might as well get my book called *"God's Inheritance in YOU!"* You will not be disappointed in reading that one. You will be blessed, I guarantee it!

So the soldier, and the one who plants a vineyard, and the one who tends a flock, they are all employed by the same person. ***And therefore I am not looking to the flock or the vineyard to sustain me.***

Even though Moses said that it's fine to do it that way, Paul says that *there is a higher way you could live in,* ***a new and living way!***

It doesn't make it wrong if all you can see right now is what Moses could see. It doesn't make it wrong to receive a salary. But I am telling you right now that there is a place in God's strategy for His *"church"* today, a place that is already prepared for us, a place of faith, where God wants us to live independent of, far removed from, a reliance upon the financial systems, far above the limits and restrictions of the financial systems of this world.

Because you see, even though it may be wonderful how it all works together and how they have worked this whole thing out to function, *it doesn't really work.* You can go and read and study your history and look back at the years of economic figures and statistics that you can lay your hands on, and you will soon discover that *it doesn't work, it will eventually fail again. It will fail you!*

But there is a way that works much better, amen. It is called grasping the faith of God, grasping that which is revealed and restored to us in Christ Jesus, *and then operating by that faith, living by the faith of God!*

I can probably add hundreds of examples, even in my own personal testimony that will confirm this word to you. But I really believe there is enough integrity in the truth of the gospel, in the things I have written and expounded on from the Scriptures in this book, as well as in my other books, *to impact your heart with the love of God, and convince you* **to trust Him fully.**

I want to make sure that you understand that your commission is of God, that you have been commissioned in love, by Mr. Love Himself, and that you have therefore been entrusted by Him with a commission *that has no strings attached.*

Listen, there are no strings attached to the true gospel! There are no strings attached to the gospel we preach!

Paul confirmed this when he said in 1 Corinthians 9:15,

"I am not writing this to you, so as to secure any such provision…"

He didn't say, *'Well, brethren, you all know that I lived for three or four years by faith and that I was really trusting God, but now that I feel I know you a little better and you have come to really know me, now let's all change what we're doing and how we are interacting, and Praise God, now we are all going to, you know, relax our faith in God, and stop trusting Him so much, and we are all going to grow up now a little more and do things a little different…'*

No, brethren, we are going to relax anyhow, amen! That's what real spiritual maturity is all about. We are going to relax in His love, and trust Him even more fully! And we are still going to have it different, amen, very different! It's going to be great!

You see, we used to think that the *"church"* was made up of maybe the one person, or perhaps the two people that the *"church"* **could afford** to have in the pulpit or to have on their staff. Hey, listen, *what a limited vision* under that old system. God wants to pioneer something in the *"church"* today, *in the heart of every saint.* It's called: **The impartation of the truth of His gospel;** *a spirit of wisdom and revelation in the knowledge of Him.*

It will release and mobilize multitudes of saints out of the comfort zone and into effective dynamic ministry!

1 Corinthians 9:18,

"What then is my reward?"

'Shame Paul, life must be really hard for you, you must have it really difficult.'

"What then is my reward?"

"Just this, that in my preaching I make the gospel free of charge, not making full use of my so-called right in the gospel. For in this way I am free from all men, yet motivated and mobilized by love, I have made myself a slave of all, so that I might win even more."

Can you now see love's compelling influence at work within his heart, compelling him to do what he does?

Chapter 6

Doing Whatever It Takes To Save Some!

Paul goes on to say in 1Corinthians 9:19,

"For those who are outside the Law…

He is talking about those who do not live under Judaism by the Law of Moses.

"For those who are outside the Law, I became as one outside the Law, yet not being outside of Law towards God, but being under the Law of Christ…"

That Law of Christ is a different Law, amen. It's a different Law from the Law of Moses.

"…so that I might win those who are outside the Law."

This is the wisdom of Paul's ministry. He is revealing that wisdom to us.

I want you to understand as you read this book that this truth that comes to your spirit through the gospel, this truth of the gospel which Paul is revealing to us here, is a radically bold truth. But don't now go and preach it and proclaim it as a radical. Don't go and preach it and proclaim it just because it is radical. I mean, don't go and say stuff just for shock value, just to get a reaction and to see people's reaction because they have never heard these things before. Don't make shock worthy, radical statements, without even attempting to qualify what you are saying and explaining it with plenty of Scripture references.

I know that the true gospel is radical and these ideas are radical and are meant to totally transform people's lives. But that can only happen when it is presented accurately and gently, in love and with understanding, without adding shock value, amen. You must learn to develop the skill to unlock people's hearts through genuine love, by being sensitive to them, showing that you genuinely care, in order to cause them to be open so that they might receive what you have to say. Otherwise you just push people away and cause them to harden their hearts towards what they do not understand and feel threatened by.

Paul preached the truth of the gospel *in such a way **that many believed,*** not in such a way that many were offended and rejected the gospel!

Our goal should always be to try and open people up to receive and embrace the gospel, not to get them to be offended and reject the gospel simply because we are puffed up in knowledge, only caring about ourselves instead of taking the time to communicate value, and trying to make them understand their value, both to you, and to God, as well as making them feel loved.

Always remember, knowledge can puff up, it can make you arrogant and prideful, *but love always seeks a way to edify, to build up and encourage,* rather than offend.

I repeat: Don't go and preach the truth of the gospel just because it is new and exciting and radical. Don't go preach it just because it is radical and you want to be a radical. No, live this Law of love; live this truth of the gospel, live the law of Christ. *Win people through genuine love,* rather than offending them and pushing them away through radical doctrine!

For the sake of outsiders, for those who do not understand God, who do not understand the gospel and are living totally wrapped up in themselves and caught up in the flesh, *relate to them, associate with them, connect with them and be a friend. Interact with them in such a way that they consider you to be like them, to be one of them, to be part of their group,* **while you yourself remain under the Law of Christ, fully aware of what you are doing, remaining fully engaged in God's strategy to win them, to win their love and affection.**

I want to make myself perfectly clear here: I am not talking about being religious and fake, full of hidden agendas and deception. Love people, and associate with people, genuinely from the heart! I am also not talking about making an excuse for compromising and joining people in their sin, just to be included by them as one of them.

I am talking about *how to truly respect and value people, how to walk in love and win people's trust and respect,* instead of walking in legalism.

You see once love has opened their hearts, their hearts will open their ears to the truth of the gospel, amen!

So do not take the teaching presented in this book and in the gospel to now go out and condemn all the pastors and ministers that are still taking a salary, and condemn all those that are sending out newsletters and posting blogs asking for support! No! What I wrote to you is for you! So that you can discern for yourself and clearly see for yourself where you operate from, and where you stand in your faith as a ministry, and as individuals, in the ministry of Jesus.

I want you to clearly see where you stand in your faith, in your trust relationship with Father God as Daddy, and with Jesus, the One who is love personified, and who has called you *to fully, accurately, represent Him and His love* in your ministry to others.

Under God's system of faith and truth, I tell you there might be many a day when you don't have a penny in your pocket. *But you will not be any the poorer.* I mean there was plenty of times when Paul had nothing to his name and everyone left him, *when he even had to sit in a dirty old prison cell.* **But he was not any the poorer** because Psalm 16 was his experience,

"In thy presence o Lord, there is fullness of joy!"

Hallelujah!

Ill repute, or good repute, it makes no difference! When they speak well of you, fine. When they speak bad of you, fine. *As long as God's opinion rules.* **God likes me, so it's all fine.**

"If God is for me who can be against me, amen?!"

Look at 1 Corinthians 10:33. Paul says,

"Just as I try to please all Men in everything I do, not seeking my own advantage, but that of the many, that they may be saved!"

Paul's heart is so clearly on display. He didn't go out to offend people with what he knew or to try and prove how radical he was for Jesus. No, he even writes to Titus in Titus 3:2-5, and he says,

"Speak evil of no one, avoid quarreling, be gentle, and show perfect courtesy towards all people, for we ourselves were once just as

they are now ...but when the goodness and kindness of God our Savior appeared, (when it was revealed to us and we grasped it,) He saved us..."

He says,

"...show perfect courtesy towards all people,"

And yet he offended many. He stood on many people's toes, **but it wasn't his heart!** He wasn't aiming for that effect, he wasn't deliberately doing it.

So you make sure that when you are commissioned, when you understand your commission, that you are not called to go out there and win some kind of word-war or some idea-war with people. *You are simply commissioned with understanding into **His love,** understanding into **that gospel,** the gospel of love.*

The fragrance of His knowledge, the fragrance of that love, the fragrance of the gospel, the fragrance of His love within you, will spread forth everywhere. *It will overcome every tribulation, every misunderstanding, every resistance,* **as long as you draw from the source that lives in your spirit, from Him who is love, from the fullness of His love and life in you.**

In 1 Corinthians 9:22, Paul goes on to say,

"To the weak I became weak..."

And now all the religious people hear that and think, *'Compromise!'*

They think, *'I compromised in order to accommodate the weak...'*

But no listen, Paul clearly says,

*"To the weak I became weak, **in order that I might win the weak."***

Not so long ago, I had the opportunity to minister in a church that was very strong on the doctrine of inner healing and deliverance. In fact, just before it was my turn to get up and speak they had the whole thing on the plumb-line in some small little presentation there, and I was so tempted to say something about the plumb-line. But I didn't. *I just got up and preached the truth of the gospel, the truth of the love of God for every single individual, **and God's message won their hearts!***

***I did that because I have more confidence in the power of the gospel, in the ministry of that truth into their spirits,** than in my attacking their wrong doctrines.*

*I know that as they meditate in and fellowship around the truth of the gospel, all those other concepts they so desperately hang on to as their identity in ministry will go the way of the Dodo, **because of the power of the gospel, because of the truth of His love. That truth prevails, the word always prevails, amen. His love always prevails; IT PREVAILS!***

I hope you can clearly see the wisdom of Paul's strategy revealed here in 1 Corinthians 9:22.

*"To the weak I became weak, **in order that I might win the weak**"*

Did Paul literally become weak? I mean, did he really become weak? Did he lose any of his strength in God?

No, he did not!

Sometimes in our conversations we are so tempted to get in there and win the argument. You might even win the argument, *but you lose the person.* What's the use of that? I remember when I first started gaining insight and revelation into the truth of the gospel (way back in the 1980's), I was so zealous. We would go out in teams and strike up conversations with anyone we ran into and we would come back all fired up and excited over how many people we offended today on the streets of South Africa, and how many people slammed their doors in our faces. Can you believe we were that foolish!? Oh yes, we were! Listen, how dumb can you get and still breathe? Ha... ha... ha...

You know, we were so proud of ourselves, but that is nothing to be proud of! So, embrace this little bit of wisdom from above: If you want to go out there and be a minister of the gospel, *represent the truth of the gospel, the truth of God's love accurately,* don't go out there trying to offend people and show them how radical you are, *'I'm just a radical rebel for Jesus!'*

No listen, rather through the open statement of the truth, rather through being written epistles, known and read by all men, rather through the demonstration of us being entrusted with His love-commission, **we minister that love to people. We impact people's conscience with love,** *and we impart that love of God to their hearts.* We are not adding any price to the gospel, we are not trying to promote ourselves as ministers and solicit their money and support, or sell *ourselves* in any way that the world approves of, trying to impress them and win their approval by being Mr. or Mrs. personality and popularity. No, rather, to the weak we become weak, in order that we might win the more.

Even to those that are still under the Law we become as those who are also under the Law still, to win them with the gospel, amen, to avoid being the very thing that offends people and causes people to stumble over the gospel.

In that way we become that level highway even in a desert land, that highway of God's love, that highway of God's approval of our spirits, and we present that gospel of approval straight, so that others may escape the wilderness upon that same highway also.

We present that highway, that gospel of approval with no crookedness, no underhandedness or hidden potholes or pitfalls, and no rough places. *So that no fault may be found with our ministry and therefore with the gospel we represent with our very lives, amen.*

*"To the weak I became weak, **in order that I might win the weak**"*

Paul goes on and says in 1 Corinthians 9:22-23,

"I have become all things to all people that I by all means might save some."

*"I do it all for the sake of the gospel, **that I may share in its blessings.**"*

That is reward enough, amen!

In Romans 9:3 Paul weeps and he says,

"I wish that I myself could be accursed, could be cut off, for the sake of my Jewish brethren, my kinsman according to the flesh…"

"I wish there was a way that I could take their place; that I could be cut off from Christ, cut off from God's favor, I will do anything, just so that they could feel included!"

But then he realizes and he says, *'But that is not possible. Christ has done enough! He has done it all! There is no way I can out-do, or out-shine Him! What is possible though is that I can become all things for all men, relating to*

*them where they are at, showing to them that I
understand where they are coming from, so
that they may receive me and embrace me as
their own,* **in order that I might reach them,
in order that I may be able to enlighten
them and show them that there is a better
way, in order that I might win them with the
gospel, in order that I might win the more!'**

*"I have become all things to all people that by
all means I may save some."*

"I do it all for the sake of the gospel, **that I may
share in its blessings.***"*

Can you see that the gospel itself, the
knowledge of the truth is Paul's reward?

And what is the gospel?

**The gospel is our acceptance in Christ
Jesus; that absolute approval, our approval
God has made known to us and fully
restored to us in Christ. That is the gospel.
And that was Paul's reward. Paul's reward
was the impact the gospel made upon his
own life,** *as well as the impact it makes on
other people's lives.* **The transformation
and wholeness and lifelong fulfillment that
the approval of God brings into his life and
into other people's lives** *is reward enough
for Paul!*

Listen, if you get anything out of this book, I
pray that you really get this: **Find your reward
in the focus of God's favor upon your life!**

You are the apple of His eye!

He loves you with everything He's got, with all He has, with His whole being!

He has been in love with you from before time began and He is not about to stop loving you now!

Sin itself was not enough to get Him to stop loving the world.

If that could not make Him stop loving us, if He would rather die than live without us, then what can separate us from His love, from His approval of us, and from the focus of His favor upon us?

Hey, go read all about it for yourself in the New Testament. Then go find your reward in the prayer closet, in your private place, in that secret place within your heart of fellowship and encounter with God. Find your reward in the truth of the gospel, in eating the finest of the wheat, and be sustained in His presence! Don't be snared to go and find your reward in a paycheck, in someone's big check that they offer you, or in someone's applause and approval that they present; someone else's recognition. **No, beloved of God, find your reward in _His_ recognition of you, in _His_ approval that _He_ has <u>already given</u> and revealed and restored to you in Christ Jesus, in that incarnation and work of redemption!**

1 Corinthians 9:24,

"Do you not know that in a race all the runners compete, but only one receives the prize? So run that you may obtain it…"

And you already have it in Christ Jesus, *just fully embrace it for yourself!* Don't run for the wrong reward, amen.

"Every athlete exercises self-control in all things…"

He basically says, *'I am not speaking here about a legalistic motivation.'* He says, they do it, they get into a competition and into self-discipline and self-denial and get legalistic, *all because of trying to obtain some perishable crown, some perishable wreath.* But we don't get legalistic. We exercise self-control of a different kind, not a discipline after the flesh, but **a faith-constraint, a love-constraint,** not in order to obtain, ***but in order to <u>maintain</u> our enjoyment of the reward we already have!***

We refuse to accept any other opinion other that the opinion of us which God revealed, the favor of God already given to us in Christ Jesus.

And therefore we yield to that love-constraint within us also, for the sake of the gospel, for the sake of <u>winning</u>, *for the <u>reward</u> of **seeing others won over by the love of God, by the favorable opinion of God towards us all as***

revealed in Christ, enjoying our reward with us!

Verse 25 again,

*"Every athlete exercises self-control in all things. They do it to receive a perishable wreath, **but we embrace an imperishable one, an imperishable reality.**"*

Paul says, verse 26 & 27,

*"I do not run aimlessly, I do not box the air. But I control myself and subdue even my body to that <u>focus</u>, to that <u>reward</u>, **to the enjoyment of that reward**, to that gospel of God, to that love-constraint, and that knowledge within my spirit **of God's approval of me and of all humanity,** revealed and <u>fully restored to us all</u> in Christ Jesus!"*

He says,

*"I do this, lest after preaching to others about it, about the gospel, about that reward, **about enjoying that approval** ...lest after preaching to others, **I disqualify myself, and see myself as falling short of it again somehow.**"*

Chapter 7

The Gospel Is For Everyone!

Just as a cross reference, let's quickly take a look at Romans 1:14.

I mean, what takes Paul to Rome? In the natural he almost didn't make it. They were shipwrecked on their way there. Do you remember that experience Luke gives an account of towards the end of the book of Acts? Even when they got washed out on that island eventually after the storm they encountered, a snake bit Paul, remember? I mean, every kind of contradiction to his journey was there, *but what took him all the way to Rome if it was not the greatest news ever,* **if not the inspiration in his spirit of the truth of the gospel, if not that reward, if not that treasure he was carrying in the earthen vessel, if not that love-constraint burning within his spirit!?**

God's word, the truth of the gospel, what he enjoyed and trusted in and carried within his spirit as a result of that truth of the gospel, *was a more secure vessel for him, a more secure covering* **than that shaky vessel that they were in in that storm. So even while he was hanging on to that plank there in the sea, in the midst of that dark storm, that plank**

was not his support, **the truth of the gospel, the love of God, the fact that he has and knows the approval of God** was his support. *The truth of the gospel, God Himself, not Man, not even the rest of the apostles in Jerusalem, was Paul's covering that protected him on all his journeys and in all his endeavors. His feet remained shod with the preparation of the gospel.*

That word *preparation* in the Afrikaans language makes it so clear. It speaks *of the attitude of your heart, the willingness, the total yieldedness of your heart to the impact and influence of that gospel.*

I can guarantee you that if the attitude of your heart is fueled by that gospel, your feet will be shod; you will be ready. You won't just sit there with it; y*ou won't sit still with it!* The gospel, the truth of the love of God for you and for all Men, *will not gather dust in your heart.* **No, you will be a sharpened sword, a polished arrow, ready in the quiver, *a vessel ready for the Master's use!***

You see, when your spirit is in such communion with God, your ministry and your life becomes more than a nice boring little program or even a wonderful invitation to just go and preach somewhere in some big place for the sake of recognition or even a big offering.

When your spirit is in such sweet communion with God, **your life and your ministry becomes one, and your life becomes your ministry,** and that ministry to others, from a heart burning with a deep love and passion, produced by the truth of the gospel, **becomes your life!**

In Romans 1:14 Paul says,

"I am under obligation, both to the Greeks, and to the Barbarians, both to the wise, and to the foolish."

Don't limit your ministry and think that, *'I've got a special ministry to the blacks, or I've got a special ministry to the whites, or I've got a special ministry to the rich, or I've got a special ministry to the poor, or I've got a special ministry to this people or to that people.'* Listen, I don't find that anywhere in the gospel, anywhere in the Scriptures, especially in the New Testament.

Praise God for specialized ministries and for people who develop an ability to communicate to children, it is wonderful. Do it, pursue it, but don't limit yourself to that. From what Paul is saying, the gospel and therefore our ministry is to both the wise and the foolish, it is to both Greeks and Barbarians, our ministry is to both Jews and Gentiles, meaning it's to both the supposedly saved and the so-called unsaved: Those who do not yet know and believe they have been rescued in Christ Jesus, in that work of redemption. So, the gospel is for everyone, for both kids and adults, for both the wise and the foolish, and therefore our ministry is as well.

Verse 15,

*"So I am eager to preach the gospel **to you also** who are in Rome."*

Paul writes to those guys in Corinth and he says in 2 Corinthians 10:14,

*"For I am not **overextending** myself **when I come to you all the way with the gospel.**"*

He came a long way with the gospel. He traveled a long journey to reach Corinth. But he was not measuring himself against those who commended themselves. He didn't have to measure himself by them and by what they had to say, amen, because he says that, *those who commend themselves are still without understanding!* **They measure themselves by themselves instead of measuring themselves in Christ Jesus. They are still without a proper understanding of the gospel; *of the measure God has measured us by* in the gospel. They do not grasp and fully understand *that approval which God has already given them as a gift in Christ Jesus.* They still measure themselves by themselves** and that is the whole problem in our day with church politics and ministerial ethics,

'You just stay on your side of the line brother, and I on mine, and that way we will do just fine laboring together in this town.'

Paul says,

*'What is the matter with you? What's the difference between me and Cephas and Apollos? As if we have any claim upon any geographical place upon this earth! Listen, are we not all co-laborers in **God's** harvest field? **Both the field and the harvest is the Lord's!**'*

You see, if it is building my own kingdom that motivates me, *then I am going to be so threatened when Apollos comes on the scene.* But if I realize that Apollos' contribution is there and necessary, to even further perfect the saints, **because God gives the growth and He gets the glory,** and we are in **His** vineyard, we are **His** soldiers, and we are tending **His** flock, *then we are no longer in any kind of competition with one another.*

That means that that whole spirit of competition, when it comes to ministry, is done away with, as far as God is concerned.

Listen; that whole territorial spirit of us competing with one another is dealt a death blow and done away with in Christ and in the love of Christ *and we are in competition with no man!*

Hallelujah!

I can guarantee you as a matter of personal testimony. I have experienced it myself in these last few years as we have gone and ministered in different churches of various denominational backgrounds, that as we go out *with the right attitude knowing that there is only one Lord, one Faith, one Baptism,* **and we are all brothers,** and as we go forth in that brotherly love and in the attitude of the very Spirit of God, **governed by His love-commission in our spirits,** *we have seen how those precious folks in their hearts received and embraced the message we preach, the truth of the gospel,* not because of any human effort, any compromised effort at unity, some organized so-called unity meetings, *but because of the witness in their hearts; in their spirits.*

You see, Paul knew that the heats of people bore witness to the truth, to the truth of God's love plan in redemption, so he didn't want anything in his conduct, any offensive or obnoxious thing, to obstruct the flow of witness, the flow of God's Spirit, the reception of God's truth and of God's love.

He says, *"I am under obligation, I am compelled and constrained and disciplined,* **to remain focused upon, and saturated with love***, and so I am eager to preach the gospel to you also who are in Rome."*

You know when I first read that in 2 Corinthians 10:13 where Paul says, *"I will keep to the limits which God has apportioned to me,"* I thought, okay, now here's Paul, he is now just going to withdraw himself and stick to a little local area because he is tired of the conflict and he doesn't want to overextend himself anymore.

But I couldn't find Paul doing that anywhere in the Scriptures, *and I had to change my own mindset about that when God began to reveal to me that **the gospel cannot be measured any smaller than the ends of the earth.***

If you are dealing with the true gospel, with God's heart for humanity, with that limit by which God measures, with that limit which God has apportioned us in the gospel, then **that limit includes the utter most parts of the earth!**

So when Paul speaks of keeping to that limit which God has apportioned us in the gospel, *he is speaking of a measure that refers to **the impact of the word, of the gospel, upon the individual.***

And so, because that **impact upon the individual** was Paul's measure he stuck to, his limit he kept to, *he was not snared by looking at large or small audiences.*

Paul did not measure the success of his ministry by large or small audiences. *He measured it only by the impact of the gospel upon the hearts of the individual.* That was the limit God had apportioned to Paul, as well as the limit apportioned to every

99

one of us in the gospel, and that is then also the very limits Paul kept to in his ministry, throughout his ministry! Thus Paul wasn't snared by large or small audiences, *because he knew that* **this gospel, this word of truth** *he was entrusted with,* **was his key to success.**

The very gospel Paul preached *was his strategy* **to impact the individual's life! And that impact, the impact of the gospel upon the heart and life of the individual was how Paul measured success in ministry.**

Once that person takes a hold of the gospel, that person might still remember way in the back of his head that Paul had something to do with it, *but the thing that now counts, the thing that has become of irreplaceable worth and value to them, is that person's own personal experience with God,* **based on the truth of the gospel they have embraced.** So in ministry we should not try and file names into a computer so that we can have a legal claim upon "x" amount of people *and measure ourselves and the success of our ministry by that list.* **No, we are in His business, employed by Him to impact the world with the gospel and restore His lost kids to Him, and to their full glory and beauty in Him!!**

Paul continues therefore there in Romans 1:16,

"For I am not ashamed of the gospel: It is the very power of God unto salvation, to everyone

who believes, to the Jew first, but also to the gentile."

And then in verse seventeen he starts talking about the righteousness of God and gets into the whole revelation of righteousness. But we are not going to get into all that in this book.

Paul's total fulfillment was in the gospel and in his experience in God, of intimate fellowship with God, afforded him by that gospel.

Chapter 8

Rejoice In The Lord Always!

Would you also go with me to Philippians 4 quickly and let's just look at some things there.

Philippians 4:4,

"Rejoice in the Lord always and again I will say; rejoice!"

To rejoice is an action word. It's a deliberate action of your spirit. That means it is not just some nice happy feeling that you wake up with one morning. Paul says, *"Re-joice"*, which means to activate the joy that is in you! Activate that joy by setting your mind on the truth of the gospel, because you know that God's joy is found *in your spirit's focus.*

When Paul writes and he says, *"Rejoice"*, he doesn't mean, *'Alright, now hang in there you know, just endure for a little while longer. Because eventually, you know, somewhere in there, somewhere in your circumstances you will finally get enough reason to rejoice. And then when you have really now enough reason to rejoice. Then is your chance, rejoice, go ahead and rejoice.'*

No, he doesn't say that. Paul says,

*"Rejoice in the Lord **always,** and **again I say to you: rejoice!**"*

He repeats himself so that we cannot possibly misunderstand what he is saying. It is always there. That joy is always there, and no matter what comes our way and comes against us, there will never be a reason not to rejoice; there will never be enough reason not to activate our joy. We can always rejoice, we can access and activate that joy in any and all circumstances, <u>always</u>, **because the truth hasn't changed. The truth of His love and favor upon us isn't going to go away!**

Hallelujah!

That joy is always there *because the gospel never changes and God's love is ever towards you.* But your rejoicing is like the water in the faucet. You can stand there with a dry mouth and look at the faucet, but until you open the thing, the water is not going to flow. So you can go ahead and stay all miserable the whole day long if you like, and keep feeling all miserable and parched and be depressed. *But when you make a choice to look away unto Jesus, the author and finisher of your faith, the One from whom perfect faith originates, **when you make a choice to look away unto Him and unto the truth of the gospel and tap into what you know to be true,** when you make a choice to activate that treasure, that joy within you, and you start rejoicing,* it's just like opening that faucet, the water is there, the joy is there. It's not sometimes, not hit and miss, not maybe, some of the time. No, it's *"... always,"* Paul says.

And then Paul gets into some wonderful teaching about not being anxious about anything, and he teaches about prayer and about the peace of God that comes **through an impartation of faith, *through the truth of the gospel that resides in your spirit.*** But I am not going to get into all that right now, but it all leads into what I want to say here. I really want to get to verse 10.

Philippians 4:10-13,

"Now I rejoice in the Lord greatly, that now at length you have revived your concern for me. You were indeed concerned for me, but you had no opportunity. Not that I complain of want, for I have learned the secret that whatever state I am in, to be content. I know how to be abased, and I know how to abound; in any and all circumstances I have learned the secret of facing plenty and facing hunger, abundance and want, and yet to remain content. I can do all things in Him who strengthens me."

"...in whatever state I am in," he says.

You better learn that in whatever state you are, there you are, *content.* Because your contentment is not because of the state you are in, or because of the country you find yourself in, or the government you are under,

but because of Him, amen! It really doesn't matter whether you live in the USA, or in Russia, or in Mozambique, amen. **Your contentment comes from knowing Jesus!** Your contentment is not because of the state you are in, but because of Him, He's the state president of your state, *finally,* amen!

Philippians 4:12,

"I know how to be abased and how to abound..."

A lot of people do not know how to abound in their spirit-man, and so abasing then becomes such a snare, and they end up with big problems, *not in their circumstances so much,* ***but in their heart; in their spirit.***

"I know how to be abased, by knowing how to abound, in any and all circumstances..."

So when Paul says this and basically refers back to verse 4, he knows what he is talking about when he says, *"Rejoice in the Lord always; and again I say to you: rejoice!"*

He says, *"...in any and all circumstances I have learned the secret of **facing** plenty and **facing** hunger, abundance and want..."*

*"...**facing** it."*

The first time I tried to preach this I got tongue tied and instead of saying: *"facing"*, I said, *'I've learned the secret of "faithing" plenty and hunger,'* and I thought to myself, *'Well that is good enough because that's exactly what you have to do.'* Ha… ha… ha…

Paul says, *"I've learned the secret of **facing** abundance **and want**"*

What was his secret?

Verse 13,

"I have learned to remain content, because I have learned to trust Him, I have learned to maintain that intimate fellowship with Him, that focus upon His love, I can do all things in Him who strengthens me!"

Another translation puts it this way,

"I can do all things through Christ who energizes me mightily from within!"

So it is clear that Paul is not drawing his energy from outward circumstances *but from the One who dwells within.* It is that indwelling Christ who enables him and anoints him, through the abiding word, through the abiding truth of the gospel, *for both life and ministry!*

Chapter 9

Not That I Seek The Gift!

Philippians 4:13-15,

"I can do all things in Him who strengthens me!"

"Yet it was kind of you to share in my trouble. And you Philippians yourselves know that in the beginning of my ministry of the gospel, when I left for Macedonia, no church, no fellowship of believers, entered into partnership with me in giving and receiving, except you only."

This church, this group of believers, this local fellowship entered into partnership with Paul and he understood the spiritual significance of their contribution to his journeys and to his ministry. He understood that their financial contribution linked them into a spiritual partnership in the ministry.

And listen, he is not writing this to secure any more provision either, believe you me. Religion has so twisted this part of the ministry of the gospel as if that's the only thing of importance. Really it has been so ingrained and hammered in over the years, and eventually people gave, but they gave because they were being manipulated to do so, and they gave reluctantly and by compulsion and under obligation. And really, being driven and pressured by that kind of motivation, they might as well have stayed out of this giving thing altogether because it doesn't mean anything to God and has very little real value and meaning even to the ones who give.

Remember that instance when Jesus sat on the side and watched the religious people under the yoke of Judaism putting in their money in the offering baskets? He didn't make any comment about how much they gave. He didn't commend any of them, but He did commend the widow woman *and made a comment about how much the rest of them all held back for themselves.* They couldn't impress Him with any size gift. He only weighed how much they kept back **because He measured their giving by what was in their hearts** and not by what was in their offering.

You see, we can't fool God by a Law-motivated giving mentality and by our Law-inspired preaching on giving. God will not be mocked because God cannot be fooled, **He knows what comes from the heart and *He knows exactly how much we give from a genuine heart,*** and how much we cling to and hold on to and reluctantly keep back because of greed or fear. He knows when our giving is *inspired,* **when it is the fruit of the gospel at work in us; when it is the fruit of love.** He knows

when it comes from freedom, when it is truly cheerful giving *and when it comes from fear.* *He knows when it is manipulated or motivated by the law, by constraint, by a sense of guilt and shame and condemnation, under obligation, or a sense of greed, motivated by a reward mentality, looking for reward, for a so-called multiplied harvest.*

As long as you are still looking at Godliness *as a means of gain,* **you are still without understanding.** **God is after your heart,** *not your wallet.* **He knows that when He has your heart, He has your whole wallet also,** *but it is not the money in your wallet that's important to Him – **you are!** **The fact that we are His children** is what's important to Him. It's the fact that we understand **we are the offspring of God,** that's what's important to Him. The fact that we understand that **we are His image and likeness on display** and that **we are indeed children of God,** and *shining forth as lights, pure and without fault, in love with our Father; with our Daddy,* in the midst of a crooked and perverse generation, *that's what's important to Him.*

Philippians 4:15,

*"No church entered into partnership, in **giving and receiving**..."*

Hallelujah, what a partnership!

*"...**giving *and* receiving**..."*

Now that doesn't mean that they are on the giving side of this equation and Paul is on the receiving side of it. No, *both Paul and they are on both sides,* because they both operate under the same Law, the Law of Christ, the Law of love, the Law of the New Creation.

Both are *"...giving and receiving,"* **both naturally and spiritually!**

Verse 16,

"...for even in Thessalonica you sent me help once and again."

*"**Not that I seek the gift**..."*

Can you see that?

He comes out very strongly again, here in verse 17,

*"**Not that I seek the gift;** but I seek the fruit which increases to your credit."*

He realizes that these people **genuinely loved him and saw him as family,** that *their genuine giving from the heart* **became a love exercise,** *a faith exercise, a trust exercise, motivated from within; from their spirits.* They began to enter into a Law: The Law of love, yes, but therefore also the Law of faith; the Law of covenant. They began to enter into the Law of God's provision, where they, *inspired by love,* release what in the natural would be considered to be their provision, but as they released it *while being motivated by that love, they discover also that God is indeed their source* **and that He becomes their provision in order to fulfill that love-desire within their hearts.**

Paul says in verse 18,

*"I have received full payment **and more**..."*

You know, just as I am sitting here writing this book, I had to go through our financial statements for this past year because of the legal proceedings one has to go through in signing a new long term lease on the building we meet in. And as I look at what we brought in and what went out the door again, and realize there is nothing left and the income does not line up with the bills ...and so you sit down and deliberately begin to think back, and you think to yourself, *'But did we need anything; did we ever lack anything?'* And then to your amazement you come to the realization that, *'No, even though we struggled at times to make ends meet, we really didn't lack, we didn't really go without.'*

Verse 18,

*"I have received full payment **and more**..."*

You see, it really makes no difference what comes in and what goes out.

*"I have received full payment **and more**..."*

If that does not sound like a testimony of contentment and fulfillment in ministry, I don't know what does!

Paul goes on to say,

*"I am filled, having received from Epaphroditus the gifts you sent, **a fragrant offering, a sacrifice acceptable and pleasing to God.**"*

Why was it acceptable and pleasing to God?

Because it was born out of love! It was born out of appreciation and thanksgiving!

Do you know what blessed Paul more than the gifts? **It was their hearts! It was the purity of their hearts, the beauty of their faith; *the genuineness of their love and friendship!***

Do you remember what happened to King David that day, while at war, when he became thirsty? His men went and risked their lives to go and fetch him some water from that particular well in Bethlehem behind enemy lines. And when they brought it to him he was so overwhelmed and overcome **by their love for him** that he poured it out *because his reward wasn't in that water.* **His reward was the level of commitment, *the level of love and friendship towards him in their hearts.***

Don't ever allow a material blessing to become your reward. It's a lie. **Live in the fulfillment of <u>genuine</u> relationships. And when those**

fall apart as they sometimes do, *live in the fulfillment of your walk with God!*

Live in the fulfillment of that and you won't be snared by any size gift that comes your way. You won't be snared by any kind of *manipulation and sweet-talk from people trying to control you,* or by any amount of money, whether it comes your way, or leaves your hands and goes out from you, *it makes no difference; you are not ruled by those things, amen!*

When Jesus saw the heart of that widow woman and He saw that small little penny that she gave drop down into that basket, He couldn't help himself. He was so blessed that He had to speak up and tell His disciples what it was that He was so blessed by; *not the size of the penny,* **but the size of that woman's love for God!** In what Jesus saw in that woman's heart, *He received infinitely more* than what could be measured by the little penny she gave.

And now, it is in this context that Paul says in Philippians 4:19,

"And my God will supply every need of yours according to His riches in glory in Christ Jesus."

So don't you go and quote this scripture out of context. It is not a nice little faith confession, a nice little positive confession concerning your needs, *'My God shall supply all my needs*

115

according to His riches in glory in Christ Jesus.' You sound like a parrot! Ha... ha... ha... We have learned that, and so we go and quote it 170 times per day *and think that we are going to get our needs met* because we want what that scripture says, we want that kind of provision, *according to God's riches up in Heaven.* But let me tell you brethren, you won't get it that way. You will only get snared into Charismatic Voodoo that way. The riches Paul is talking about is not first of all up in heaven somewhere. God's riches are within you! Let's read it in context, okay?

Paul says, *"**My** God..."* he is not making a confession here for his own lack, is he? No, he is not. He has already said, *"I have received full payment ...**and more!**"* **He is speaking from a place of abundance, not lack!**

A brother phoned me the other day and proceeded to tell me how depressed he is that his faith isn't working. He said, *'I have sat under the most positive Charismatic word for many, many years now, and I still lack!'* He has made all the right confessions and given all kinds of money in offerings, *but he is still poor!* And my heart totally went out to him because he has been lied to and manipulated. You see, *we miss it with faith **if we miss the teaching of righteousness by faith.*** Faith is not about all you can get. That is not what faith is about. ***It's about enjoying righteousness by faith. If faith is not about righteousness, about being face to face with God,*** about *enjoying intimate fellowship there,* **about** *being in love with Jesus,* **then it's not faith, then it's got nothing to do with faith.**

We can be the most positive people in the country, **but if we don't understand our righteousness, if we don't actually have intimate fellowship with God, if we don't enjoy a constant, sustaining, intimate encounter with God,** *if we do not become infatuated with the love of God for us,* **abiding in Him, face to face with Him, and Him abiding in us,** *we miss it!*

We can learn to build the largest barn and focus our faith on that, and we can focus on it until we accomplish it, but Jesus says, *"You who build your large barn, you are a fool!"* He says, *"Rather provide yourself with a small purse, keep your money liquid and trade with it,* (trade with the gospel), *stay mobile and do business* (stay engaged in the ministry of the gospel, in the giving and receiving that result from it) *till I come."*

How large a barn must you build to accommodate your future, pastor, or apostle, or whatever it is you call yourself to try and boost your ego?

Listen; you cannot build a barn large enough to accommodate your destiny!

Your destiny is not that barn you are building! *Your inheritance is way larger than that barn!*

117

So stop telling your soul, *'Just be at ease soul, there is plenty of grain laid up here for many years, so be at ease.'* If you would only listen, you would hear your soul saying back to you, *'But I can't eat that stuff! You are poor towards God! Man shall not live by bread alone, but by that eternal Word, that unchanging truth of God's love; that gospel that proceeds from the mouth of God!'*

That Judas spirit has snared many pastors and many people in multitudes of churches today, but God wants to release them! I know it's a strong word I am penning down for you to read in this book, *but it is high time for God's kids to be released!* And as you get released, God wants to release many through your testimony, amen, as you begin to live in the richness and the wealth of your Father's provision made for you in Christ Jesus, to restore your righteousness, to restore your innocence, to restore you to intimate fellowship with Daddy, from a pure heart, undistracted, *fully reconciled and **in love with Him who is love.***

That's God's provision, that's the place Jesus went and prepared for us in His work of redemption, *a place in the Father's bosom.* **That's what we were originally designed for, nothing less, and nothing else!**

As you live in your Father's provision in Christ Jesus, *you discover that you are the apple of your Daddy's eye.* You are your Daddy's kid, knowing, knowing fully; *intimately knowing that*

your Father knows that you need all these things.

So, don't be anxious! Your anxiety links you up to the systems of this world. Your anxiety tells you, *'You better build yourself a bigger barn, or at least some kind of barn, because next year might not be as good as this year!'* You can go read all about it there in Luke Chapter 12, about the man with the big barns.

Later on in that same chapter Jesus says, *'I counsel you, provide yourselves with purses that do not grow old.'* Hallelujah! He was talking about the content of the gospel. But we do not have time to get into all that in this book. You can just go and study it there for yourselves if you like.

And now Paul says, Philippians 4:19 & 20,

"My God will supply every need of yours, according to His riches in glory, in Christ Jesus…"

That phrase, *"according to His riches in glory"* speaks of the riches of His *"doxa"* of His *"dokeo",* of His **opinion and approval** of you and I, *which He has already given to us, and revealed to us in Christ Jesus!*

Those *"riches"* that *"glory"*, **are already deposited within us by the truth of the gospel,** *ready to be enjoyed, ready to be drawn from and drawn upon in times of need.*

"To our God and Father be glory for ever and ever. Amen!"

Chapter 10

Love And Joy In Overflow!

Let's quickly go to 2 Corinthians 8:1 & 2,

*"We want you to know brethren about the grace of God which is being shown in the churches of Macedonia, for in a severe test of affliction, **their abundance of joy,** in spite of their extreme poverty, **have overflowed in a wealth of liberality on their part.**"*

What was their secret?

*"...**their abundance of joy**..."*

How did they show forth the grace of God? I mean, how was the grace of God *they were enjoying in their inner-man* being shown among them? Through *"...their abundance of joy..."* which *"...overflowed in a wealth of liberality..."*

Listen, these things do not make sense to the natural man. I mean, how can you have an abundance of joy which overflows in a wealth of liberality *while going through a severe test of affliction and facing extreme poverty?*

Where did they get this abundance of joy from *if not from the truth of the gospel; the truth of*

God's immense love for them revealed in Jesus, and His full embrace of them in the successful work of redemption, as His kids!?

Do you still remember what Paul wrote to the Philippians in Philippians 4:4?

"Rejoice in the Lord every now and again when you finally get your next paycheck…"

Ha… ha… ha… No!

*"Rejoice in the Lord **always!**"*

*"And again I say, **always rejoice!**"*

Paul said, *"I've learned the secret."* **And this church, these believers, obviously *learned the same secret!***

Under a tremendous test of affliction, in extreme poverty even, **there still remained a wealth in their spirits that overflowed in abundance. *It manifested in a wealth of liberality!***

Liberality is measured by what's in your heart, by what your heart full of love and full of trust in God who loves you, has determined to give, amen, not by what you can afford to give.

Now verse 3,

"For they gave according to their means, as I can personally testify," says Paul.

And all those who know the Law would say, *'Praise God, that is right brother Paul, we can all testify to the blessing available in that measure!'*

But here it comes; *here is the grace of the New Testament on display:*

*"For they gave according to their means, as I can testify, **and beyond their means, of their own free will**…"*

When they didn't yet understand the grace of God, when they didn't yet grasp the gospel, and they were instructed under the Law, under the Old Covenant, to give a portion of their income, called: The Tithe; that was an Old Testament doctrine. But now you see, the New Testament says, *"Present your bodies a living sacrifice…"* And believe you me, **if your fulfillment in life is now what His portion is inside of you,** *then you are no longer limited to a limited blessing; y*ou are no longer limited to Tithing.

Praise God, you no longer have to sit there and count off every penny, and get all legalistic about the exact portion that you're giving. *But instead, now you are living in His wealth, **in the wealth of His love for you, and of His favorable opinion and approval of you, and you are set free, and you find yourself giving even beyond your means!***

Hallelujah!

If you give according to your means, it speaks of a natural calculation, a natural measure. But when you give beyond your means *it speaks of a spiritual measure, a supernatural measure,* **it speaks of the measure of His love-deposit in you because you carry in your spirit *a treasure beyond measure,* a deposit of His truth and of His love and therefore of His faith!**

It is that *treasure* that becomes our motivation in giving. Otherwise, if you are going to budget your giving, you are going to be snared. *But rather give according to the Spirit of God, the Spirit of love and abundance of joy and enjoyment in God, who resides within your spirit.*

Paul says there in the next chapter that everyone must make up his own mind. It actually says in the Greek that every person must be determined *in their own spirit;* ***they must listen to the motivation that comes from within their own heart.***

2 Corinthians 8:3-5,

*"For they gave according to their means, as I can testify, **and beyond their means, of their own free will, begging us earnestly for the favor of taking part in giving** towards the relief of the saints,"*

"...and this they did, not as we expected, but they first gave themselves to the Lord and then also to us by the will of God;"
124

"...*begging us earnestly for the favor of taking part in giving*..."

Today, because of the legalistic and religious mentalities ruling in many believers' hearts and minds, we have this whole thing switched around. Today we have the ministers, *"...begging earnestly..."* But in this scripture, because of Paul's teaching, *because of the impact of the gospel, because of the impact of the love of God, and because of that same love of God now quickened and unleashed within their hearts,* it was the people who began to beg Paul earnestly for the opportunity to give, for the favor of taking part in the offering, *because they were so set free by the love of God proclaimed in the truth of the gospel!*

In our day we have been cheated through a Judas spirit in leadership, and it's *also been imparted to us.* It was Judas who carried the money bag all the time, *but he was a bean counter.*

2 Corinthians 8:3-5,

"...*begging us earnestly for the favor of taking part in giving* towards the relief of the saints."

*"...and this they did, **not as we expected,** but they first gave themselves to the Lord and then also to us by the will of God."*

***Grasping the love of God** made them understand the will of God; it made them understand that appeal in the gospel to present their bodies to the Lord, a living sacrifice.*

You see, this thing called ministry wasn't something that was outside of their comfort zone that they moved into and out of from time to time, **but their ministry was themselves given over to the God who loves them deeply, and therefore also to the proclamation of that gospel and its global impact.**

Let's also look at 2 Corinthians 9:6,

"The point is this: He who sows sparingly will also reap sparingly, and he who sows bountifully will also reap bountifully..."

How do you measure sparingly and how do you measure bountifully?

Verse 7 says,

"Each one must do as he has determined in his spirit, or with his heart, not reluctantly (as being forced to give)*, or under compulsion* (being manipulated or coxed with the promise of some kind of reward) *for God loves a cheerful giver..."*

So it is your joy, your level of love and passion for what you are involved in, the

pleasure it brings you, which determines the measure of sparingly or bountifully.

Sparingly or bountifully has got nothing to do with how many dollars you have and are willing to part with, *but it has everything to do with how much pleasure, how much joy is behind your giving.* **Your joy measures your abundance!**

2 Corinthians 9:8-10,

"And God is able to provide you with every blessing (every pleasure) *in abundance!"*

"So that you may always have enough of everything and may provide in abundance for every good work."

"Just as it is written, 'He liberally scatters abroad and gives to the poor (poor in spirit, not just poor in the natural, that too amen, but He gives to the poor, to bring them out of their poverty of spirit). His righteousness endures forever'."

"Now, He who supplies seed to the sower, and bread for food, will supply and multiply your seed, and increase the harvest of your righteousness."

How is that for a New Testament principle? *Sowing from righteousness,* and not from the Law! **Sowing from your knowledge and enjoyment of your righteousness will cause**

you to reap a harvest, *an even greater, ample enjoyment of that righteousness.*

Can you also see the difference between seed and bread? Don't ever eat your **seed!** You can even cast your *bread* upon the waters, and it will return to you, ***but never eat your seed!*** Everything that God gives you is both seed and bread. Let the Spirit of God show you which portion is seed and which portion is bread.

I can personally testify that this has made such a difference in our own lives as we began to practice this. It is called walking by faith or *trusting God,* developing a sensitive ear and listening to the voice and leading of His love and of His Spirit within you. We began to practice this as a habit years ago. During those days we still did not receive any kind of support from anyone. Actually I was still a missionary in Southern Africa, going from village to village in Malawi and ministering in schools in the poor areas of South Africa when God began to challenge me on the seed and bread principle and about walking *in **trust** and faith.* Sometimes, trust me, **I only had seed, but I kept trusting God and I sowed that seed,** *knowing that it's my last little bit of money, or my only pair of dress shoes, or my only sweater, or my only something.* **But I kept being obedient to His love alive within me and developing that trust relationship with the Holy Spirit** and every time I needed it, *the bread would show up,* guaranteed! So, quite often I would have nothing, *but I never went without.* **God always provided.**

King David said, *"I have been young, and I have been old, but never have I seen the righteous forsaken or their seed out begging bread."*

You won't ever need to beg, I guarantee it. *Just trust God, trust His love for you and let God teach you the secret to face plenty and hunger, to face poverty and wealth, to face it with faith,* **with the truth of His love for you, and therefore with full <u>trust</u> in Him, burning in your heart!**

2 Corinthians 9:11,

"You will be enriched in every way, for great generosity, which, through us, will produce thanksgiving to God (by those who see your heart, and God's love for them on display through you, when they become recipients of your generosity).*"*

Verse 15 says,

"Thanks be to God for His inexpressible gift (joy unspeakable and full of glory – inexhaustible)!"

Thank you Jesus!

Hallelujah!

Chapter 11

Never Thirst Again!

Let's go to one more scripture in John 4. It says there in John 4:4-6 that,

"Jesus had to pass through Samaria. So He came to a city in Samaria, called Sychar, near the field that Jacob gave to his son Joseph."

"Jacob's well was there, and so Jesus, wearied as He was with His journey, sat down beside the well. It was about the sixth hour."

Now Jesus was weary, so don't feel condemned when in your going you also get tired and feel weary in your body. And here Jesus was, and He sat there next to this well. And He was weary and thirsty, but He didn't have anything that would enable Him to draw water from the well. So He just sat there next to this well, anticipating that eventually somebody would come to draw water from the well and then He could ask them for a drink for Him and His disciples as well.

I want you to see that Jesus lived a very practical life. He didn't live some supernatural super-human life. He wasn't there trying to do a miracle and commanding the water to come forth supernaturally. No, He was living a normal life and He was very practical in His reasoning here as a man. He must have told His disciples, *'Hey, look you guys, I am hungry and I am sure you guys must be getting hungry too, so why don't you guys go in to town and buy us some food, and I'll just wait here for you guys, because I am slum wore out from our long journey and all the ministering we've been doing. I am sure that before long someone will come along with something to draw water with, and I can probably talk them into giving me some, and I'll save some then for you guys as well. So hurry up and go; I'll be here when you get back.'*

Sometimes ministry is very practical, so, don't go spend a bunch of money on food when you aren't hungry, and when you're tired, take a break if you need to. But if you get hungry and you have money to spend on food then take care of your physical body and don't abuse it. I mean, they had a long dusty journey, so Jesus sits down at the well to rest, and he doesn't feel condemned about it, *as if the Father expects more out of Him than what He can give.* No man, He was flesh and blood just like us, and He understood the physical limitations of the human body and its need for food and water and rest.

Now verse 7 says, *"There came a woman of Samaria to draw water."*

That woman was sent of God, amen. I mean Jesus was so tired and so thirsty, and even though He wanted to rest He couldn't quite rest, because can you imagine being thirsty and sitting right next to the faucet, or the well in this case, and yet not being able to drink any water. It's even greater torture if you can hear the water down in the well, or perhaps smell and see the water down there, and He could. He could hear it and perhaps see it and smell it. I am sure He could drop a stone down into that well and hear it go, "Plonk!" in the water if nothing else. He could have done that just to see if Jacob's old well still had any water in it after all those years. *We don't know, we weren't there, but just let your imagination go there with me.*

So, Jesus was parched. Maybe the enemy even tried to challenge Him by saying something like, *'Hey, if you're the Son of God, why sit here, just believe God and extend your arm all the way down and get you some of that water to drink.'* Like one of the Fantastic Four or something! Ha… ha… ha…

No, listen, He sat there and had to wait for someone to come, and he hoped they would be kind to Him. *He was limited to a meatbox like ours.* So He just sat there and He was thirsty until the woman came. And she was there to draw water, and so Jesus said,

'Praise God Lady, I am so glad you came, I almost died of thirst sitting here waiting on you to come and help me.' Ha… ha… ha…

The scripture says, *"Jesus said to her, 'Give me a drink.'"* I mean our translations makes it sounds so blunt and so rude. It is the first thing Jesus says to her, and He demands, *'Woman give me a drink!'* Ha… ha… ha…

No, I don't believe that is how the conversation went, so relax Max; don't take the Scriptures so literally some times. But let's read on, it says,

"For His disciples had gone away into the city to buy food. The Samaritan woman said to Him, 'How is it that you, a Jew, ask a drink of me, a woman of Samaria? For you Jews, have no dealings with us Samaritans.'"

Can you see that this woman's mind wasn't renewed? She probably though that for any man to talk to her, *especially if he is a Jew, he must be interested in her or something.* Can you imagine what the town's people thought after she had a drink of the water Jesus gave her and she left her jar lying there and she came running back to town so excited, telling everyone she met in the street, *'I found a man…'* They must have thought, *'Oh, another one? You had five already! Ha... ha... ha... What makes this one so special?'*

Let's actually read what happened there, John 4:7,

"There came a woman of Samaria to draw water, and Jesus said to her, 'Give me a drink.' And the woman said to Him, 'How is it that you,
134

a Jew, ask me for a drink? **For you Jews have no dealings with us Samaritans.**'"

I fully believe that her question, her politically and racially, religiously charged question and accusation *challenged Jesus' true identity.* It challenged the Spirit of God that resided in him. He was hungry and tired and thirsty, just being a mere man, a natural man. But when she made that accusation and asked Him that question, it challenged His true identity, the truth of who He really was in His spirit-identity as the Son of God. *You see, that spirit-truth, that powerful spiritual dynamic got stirred up in Him, in His consciousness, and the Spirit of God was quickened within His spirit, and that Holy Spirit very much alive inside of Jesus then gave Him an opportunity to witness to this woman.*

And all you Pentecostals out there can just picture how Jesus may have felt the goose-bumps right then and there as a sign to Him to minister to this woman. And He may have felt like, *'This is a divine strategic opportunity.'* Ha... ha... ha...

But somehow I don't think so. Because He was hungry, thirsty, and He was tired. So I imagine, just like with us, His spirit was just dormant within Him, fast asleep. The furthest thing from His mind right then was another ministry opportunity. He was not in the mood in that moment. He was not all spiritual and praying in tongues or anything.

135

But when that woman asked that question, the Spirit of God leaped within His spirit, reminding Him of eternal spirit-truth, spirit-reality, and suddenly who He really was and is in His spirit-man came rushing to the forefront of His consciousness. *Suddenly He realized afresh His identity and His commission.*

The Jews and the Samaritans were so separated, religiously and culturally and politically. They still are today. But He knew that He came in God's time, in the fullness of time, to break down every wall of hostility, and to reconcile all things to Himself, and restore it to its original design and its proper order.

Suddenly it was burning afresh and anew in His heart that it's the fullness of time, it is high time for all Mankind to be restored to their original design and proper spiritual order, to be reconciled to God and one another, *by grasping their Daddy's love for them and their true spirit-identity.*

And so a greater unction, a greater compulsion, a greater commission than hunger and thirst took hold of His spirit. He realized afresh and anew that this was God's time, today was the day of salvation, and He must have said within Himself, *'I hear You, My Father; I hear Your voice within me. I hear You and I know what You are saying. I am indeed here for bigger business than just getting my thirst quenched and having my stomach fed!'*

136

Verse 10,

"He said to the woman, 'If you knew the gift of God, and who it is that is saying to you, 'Give me a drink,' you would have asked Him, and He would have given you living water.'" (Jesus was that gift and what God came to accomplish and say to humanity, in that gift, is that living water!)

"If you knew the gift of God…"

'If you knew that gift you wouldn't be so racial, so naturally-minded; so conscious of you being a Samaritan and me being a Jew, you wouldn't be so conscious of humanity's natural identity!'

'If you weren't so religiously confused and ignorant, so politically brainwashed and you only knew the gift God wants to give you to enjoy, and who it is that is saying to you, 'Give me a drink,' you would have asked Him, and He would have given you living water.'

That well of life in Jesus was quickened and stirred up and ready to gush forth. You see, when you are familiar with that voice inside of you, when you are used to that, *"qavah",* when you are used to fellowshipping with God, with His thoughts, with His voice, with His person, *intertwining yourself with the Spirit of God,* **that strengthening, that encounter, that well can be quickened again in an instant!** When you *"qavah"* with God in your spirit, *your weariness goes.* I am telling you, you might be as tired as anyone in any given circumstance, *but your* *weariness goes, and that spirit you have from God begins to leap inside of you and your heart begins to burn with truth, with the love of God for all Mankind, for every single individual, and that river inside of you begins to flow.*

And so Jesus instantly began to forget about His own needs. I am suddenly reminded also of the words of Paul when he said, *"We gladly suffer the loss of all things, and we endure all things for the sake of the gospel."*

John 4:10-14,

"If you knew the gift of God, and who it is that is saying to you, 'Give me a drink,' you would have asked Him, and He would have given you living water.'"

"The woman said to Him, 'Sir, the well is deep and you have nothing to draw with, where would you get this living water from, are you greater than our father Jacob who gave us this well and drank from it himself, him and his sons and his cattle?'

*"Jesus said to her, 'Everyone who drinks of this water will thirst again, **but whoever drinks of the water that I shall give him will never thirst;** the water that I shall give him will become in him a spring of water welling up to eternal life."*

I believe that in that moment Jesus again experienced what He did in the wilderness when for forty days He stayed without water and without bread, *but He was sustained in His fellowship with God.* He knew of a different well to drink from. He knew of a well that wasn't too deep to draw from, a well, **a rejuvenating, energizing source of life that was always available and which resides within His spirit.** *And this woman's need opened the door for ministry and as He began to minister to her, **the well within her was also quickened.*** And I am giving you a secret today, a key.

You see, there will be times in your life and ministry when you feel weary, and those times are ideal times for the enemy to tempt you and try and snare you. He knows how to mess with your emotions and you will begin to feel, *'Woe is me, here I am sitting somewhere desolate, and I don't have anything to draw water with for myself, and I have no one to minister to me, and I don't have any food to eat, and I am alone, and I had to walk all this way just to get nowhere,'* and you can start feeling inadequate and you can easily start to feel sorry for yourself and begin to throw a little pity party!

Listen, in that situation consider it an ideal situation to first of all stir yourself up with truth, with the truth of who you are in your spirit-man, and with the truth of your Daddy's unequivocal, eternal love for you, and then start ministering on purpose to someone else. It can be anyone. It doesn't matter who, just grab the first person that comes your way. When you feel at your lowest physically, mentally, and emotionally, when you feel like you've given all you've got, when you feel like there is nothing left to give, *make a conscious demand upon the well of truth and love and spirit-life and anointing that resides within you!* I have often practiced that **and seen God's supernatural release and restoration of my soul from within my own spirit.**

This principle combined with the principle of seed and bread are the two principles that released me in ministry, and released me financially, *and launched me **to be able to go to the nations.*** When I had nothing, I said, *'God where's the seed, give me seed, for You are the One who gives seed to the sower and bread for food, and if there is no bread for food right now then give me seed to sow.'* And sure enough **I would find seed to give.** And when there were no ministry doors opening, no ministry opportunities I would say, *'God there is spiritual need all around me, where is the next place, the next person. Where do You want me to go and minister and share the gospel, and He'd show me, and I got up, and I went, and I ministered and shared the gospel.'*

And it is clear what began to happen as Jesus began to minister the gospel to this woman: *she began to drink.*

And then the Spirit of God revealed to Jesus that this woman was so unfulfilled in her life. She went through five husbands already and still she could not find fulfillment in life.

John 4:15-26,

*"The woman said to Him, 'Sir, give me this water, **that I may not thirst, nor have to come and draw from here ever again**.'"*

"So Jesus said to her, 'Go call your husband, and come here together so that I may share something special, this living water, with both of you.'"

"But the woman answered Him, 'I have no husband.'"

"Then Jesus said to her, 'You are being truthful with me now, for you have had five husbands already, and even the one who is with you now still doesn't satisfy and fulfill that deep longing, crying out from inside of you for a love that is even greater than what any man can give you!'"

Verse 19,

"The woman said to Him, 'Sir, I perceive that you are a prophet. So let me ask you a spiritual question, because I am so religiously confused: Our forefathers worshiped on this mountain and yet you Jews say that only in Jerusalem is the place where we all ought to worship.'"

In other words: *"I've got my background, my religious persuasion and you've got yours. I've got my religion and you've got your religion. I've got my church and you've got yours.*

*Who's right and who's wrong? Which church
should I go to then?"*

Verse 21,

*"But Jesus said to her, 'Woman, I am telling
you the truth. So believe me when I say, the
hour that has been prophesied as coming,
when neither on this mountain, not in
Jerusalem, will people have to worship
anymore, according to the ignorant religious
traditions handed down by their forefathers,
that hour is here, it has arrived."*

Listen; our forefathers have all missed it,
amen. They all have had some glimpses of the
truth, of what is real, but for the most part they
have all had the cat by the tail!

Jesus basically says to that woman that,

*'Even though religion is Man's best guess
about God and how to interact with Him, and
they were all sincere, yet they have all missed
it in their guesses, even us Jews as well,
Nevertheless'* he says, *'The Jews knew a little
bit more about what they were talking about
than most, because...'*

Verse 22,

"You Gentiles worship (believe and admire and
promote) *what you do not even know or
understand; but we Jews at least worship*
(believe, celebrate and promote) *what we
know; at least we do know and understand that*
142

*Mankind's rescue is from the Jews. But allow Me to let you in on a secret which not even My people, the Jews, know and understand: The day that was coming **is now here,** when the true worshipers* (those who know and understand truth accurately; those who grasp the truth about God and about themselves and about others also, and about life) *will worship* (they will believe and admire and celebrate and promote) *the Father, in spirit and truth* (...in spirit dimension and reality, according to their true spirit-identity)*, for such* (people with true revelation and understanding into the truth, so they may properly accurately relate to God, *for such*) *the Father seeks* (He desires after that kind of relationship with Man)*."*

Verse 24,

"God is spirit, (...and man is spirit also; Man is brought forth from within God, we are His image and likeness, His offspring, His children) *and therefore, those who worship Him, must worship Him in spirit, from that true spirit-identity truth, and from that reality."*

Verse 25,

*"The woman then said to Him, 'I know that Messiah is coming, and it is said, and this I actually do believe **that when He comes, He will show us all things**.'"*

*"To that Jesus immediately responded and said to her, '**I am Him**.'"*

As we read, we can see how Jesus was stirred up in His spirit-identity and was now fully conscious of the spirit-realm and ministering to this woman from that other realm, from that spirit-dimension. And we can see how *the Spirit of God strengthened and sustained Jesus* as He ministered to her.

And that women, so excited, so fulfilled, as she was grasping spirit-truth, the living water Jesus was sharing with her, perhaps now even forgetting to get a drink for herself or for Jesus, ran back to the town to tell her friends what had just happened to her. And it was just about then during that time that the disciples returned and we read from verse 31,

John 4:31-35,

"Meanwhile the disciples besought Him and said, 'Rabi, eat.' But He said to them, 'I have food to eat (I have been strengthened from a source) *that you* (in your natural thinking) *do not know.'*

"So the disciples said to one another, 'Has anyone brought Him food?' But Jesus said to them, 'My food is to do the will of Him who sent Me, and to accomplish His work. Do not say in your hearts, 'There are yet four more months, and then comes the harvest.' I tell you, lift up your eyes, and see how the fields are already ripe unto harvest.'"

I mean, Jesus could have just entered into an ordinary conversation with them there, just like
144

they did when they talked on the journey and they were all tired and they said to Jesus, *'All right Jesus, You wait here at the well and we'll go into town and buy some food.'* But no, when they came back, Jesus began to speak words from a different dimension, from a different perspective, from a different Source.

His heart was burning within Him and He saw the harvest. He saw the Jews and the Samaritans divided, and He became so aware of His commission, and knew that He had received the ministry of reconciliation. And as He began to minister to that woman **from that well of truth and reality within Him, suddenly His thirst went, suddenly His weariness went, His tiredness went, even His hunger went, and He sustained, not only Himself and that woman, but He sustained that whole town with the words of salvation.** And that woman drank of that water He gave her, of that gospel, of that good news, of that message crammed chock full of spirit-truth, *and her whole world changed.* And she ran *because she drank from a new well, and found a new Husband you see,* **the real and living God, her Maker, her Daddy, her lover,** and that whole town came under the influence of her ministry and her testimony, *and under the impact of Jesus' words to her.*

You see, that's the impact of your fellowship with God in the truth of the gospel. That's the potential of God's commission upon your life!

You know, God is not sending you out on your own now, leaving you to work out how you are going to do it financially, you know, and how much money you're going to need to get there, and then how much money you are going to need to survive there, to be sustained there, and then how much money you are going to have to set aside to give regularly, and how you are going to work it all out, you know.

'Let's all work on some nice gimmicks together and figure out, how is the best way, you know, how exactly are we going to write the most effective newsletter, so that you successfully can now really move the people, you know your contacts and prospective givers, so that you can now really move them to tears so they can more readily support your ministry.'

No man, that is not it! It really doesn't work that way! Oh, they try to make it work that way, but in the end it doesn't really work either. You can go and ask those poor precious Christian people who are trying to implement those things, and they will be quick to let you know how they are suffering under consistent, tremendous financial strain, and worry and anxiety, and many of them can't take it. *And that's why there are about eight pastors a day right now leaving the ministry according to the latest statistics.*

Listen God wants to deposit truth into your spirit that will take your ministry far beyond any budgeting. If you stay prepared, with the gospel burning in your heart, ready in your spirit to make known the gospel with clarity, because of your personal walk with Him, because of your personal encounter with Jesus in the Scriptures and in the closet, in the privacy of your heart, drinking from that spiritual fountain, *those rivers of living water would remain available, ready to flow and be released from within you; from out of your innermost being, **from out of the abundance of your heart.***

Living in the overflow, living in that constant state of readiness, enjoying that abundance, that fullness, *will turn any opportunity into a pulpit, into a speaking opportunity, and you find yourself ministering one on one, or to a group, or a crowd, or whatever door opens up to you.*

Living in that fulfillment of fellowship with God, in that abundance and fullness and overflow, you begin to see that *the needs of the world out there are bigger than your own personal needs now.* You will begin to see that the thirst of that woman or that man in front of you, *and the family and the neighborhood and the nation they represent, are bigger than your own personal needs.*

You see, God wants to sustain you with manna from heaven *and then you'll want to eat His meat called ministry.* You see, that is what Paul was talking about, that's what Paul meant when he said what he did in 1 Corinthians 9:14,

"He who preaches the gospel shall live by the gospel."

I am telling you what; if you are hungry for more, first stir yourself up in the truth of the gospel. Feed yourself first with redemption realities, spirit-identity realities, with the love of God for you personally, and then get up off of your couch or your pew and go and preach, go and share the gospel of the love of God for you and for all people. And I am not talking about waiting or wanting some pulpit opportunity, there are plenty of individuals who need their spiritual ears and eyes opened and enlightened with the truth of God's love revealed in the gospel.

If you become conscious of your own needs, get your eyes off of yourself by focusing on Jesus, on the truth of the successful work of redemption, and on His love for you, on your Daddy's love for you, and then go and find yourself a hospital or somewhere where there are lots of people that need ministering to. Go and find yourself others to minister to instead of sitting there with your eyes on yourself and your own needs.

Listen, begin to just recognize again your sonship, *your oneness with Him who is love,* and then begin to recognize again also afresh and anew your commission in Christ Jesus to be His representative, His minister, a minister of reconciliation, a minister of that good news. *Begin to recognize the gift that is within you, the gift of the Holy Spirit, the gift of God Himself in all His fullness abiding within you!*

The people all around you in this world can drink all the water they want, all the water they can stomach from the well of politics and society and culture and religion they are currently drinking from, and they will still be thirsty. *But when you come and you connect with them, spirit to spirit, heart to heart, and you minister to them out of the abundance of your heart, out of the abundance of your spirit, out of the truth of the successful work of redemption, out of the abundance of the love of God for them, and for you, and for all people, you'll never lack. And if they have ears to hear, neither will they.*

You will never lack, hallelujah, because you are His soldier, not your own, and you are not getting entangled in civilian pursuits, but you busy yourself with genuine, intimate fellowship with God in the Spirit, and with your commission and assignment as a soldier. And you refuse to get into moaning and groaning about wages, like perhaps the other soldiers you run with or you run into on the field do, because you know you are working in **His** vineyard, and **He** sustains you, hallelujah, even in tending **His flock; tending to His lost kids who need to be loved, and who needs to** find their way home to the bosom of their Father.

Listen, I say again: **You will discover fulfillment in ministry just drinking from that well within you that won't run dry;** *just simply drinking from that well for yourself, first.*

Don't try and give others a drink *if you are not drinking from it yourself first.* You cannot give what you do not have; *what you do not personally draw from and enjoy.*

John 4:36-42,

"He who reaps (what has been sown in the work of redemption) ***receives*** (its) ***wages,*** *and gathers* (delicious) *fruit for* (the enjoyment of) *eternal life,* ***so that sower and reaper together may rejoice."***

"For here the saying holds true, 'One sows while another reaps.'"

"I sent you ***to reap*** *that for which you did not labor; others have labored* (the prophets of old, declaring in Scripture the fulfillment of prophecy; the fulfillment of the work of redemption), *and you have entered into* (the enjoyment of the fulfillment of) *their labor."*

"Many Samaritans from that city believed in Him because of the woman's testimony, 'He told me all that I ever did.' So when the Samaritans came to Him, they asked Him to

150

stay with them; and he stayed there two days. **And many more believed <u>because of His word; his message</u>.** *They said to the woman,* **'It is no longer because of your words that we believe, for we have heard for ourselves,** *and we know that this man is indeed the Savior of the world.'"*

Peter writes in 1 Peter 1:8 about the love we have for Jesus and he says,

"Without having seen Him (in the flesh) *you love Him; though you do not see Him* (with your natural eyes) *you believe in Him and rejoice with unutterable and exalted joy."*

We may not see and know Him after the flesh anymore, **but we have seen Him, and do see Him still, amen.** Because in 1 John 1, John says that,

"That which we have heard and seen and looked upon, we have also touched with our hands, **those realities concerning the word of life became a tangible reality to us.** *That life was made manifest, and* **it is made manifest to us even now still,** *even* **within us,** *in our fellowship with the Father and with His Son Jesus Christ, in the Holy Spirit, and* **our joy is full.** *And so this word of life,* **the very life of it,** *that Spirit,* **that Spirit to spirit enjoyment, that spirit-dimension life,** *we now make known to you, and so also* **impart to you,** *so that* **your joy may be full also."**

Listen; let that be all the visible evidence you need for your commission. Taste and see that the Lord is good. Taste the word, taste the message; *be a first partaker of the gospel, and* <u>*see*</u> *for yourself.* **Experience Him for yourself, sweet intimate fellowship with Him! Let that genuine fellowship with Him** *commission you and propel you* **into a local and global ministry!**

Oh Hallelujah!

Thank you Father!

The lines have indeed fallen to us in pleasant places!

The Lord Himself is our portion!

Whom do we have in heaven but You, o Lord!

There is nothing upon this earth that we desire besides You!

Father, we do not want to draw from any other source. We don't want to drink and be moved by any other fountain, any other fulfillment than our walk with You daily in the garden, in the Eden of our hearts, enjoying the fullness of that Paradise of God within us, measured by the completeness of your labor enduring the cross and reappearing from the grave, victorious over death, in the resurrection, raising us up with You to newness of life!

Thank you Father that *we are no longer* **laboring for the reward or the applause of people;** some recognition that merely lasts for a moment!

And Father, we are not serving to impress anyone, not even You, *because You are so impressed with us from all eternity past already!*

Thank you that we owe You nothing, that what You did for us, You did *as a gift,* and that You therefore are already impressed with us in the greatest way possible.

You always have been, and You always will be!

Thank you that Your full approval and favor is our portion already in Christ Jesus.

Thank you that we enjoy full acceptance in the Beloved!

Father I thank you for the necessity, and the compelling love of God that is laid upon us, and awakened within us, within our spirits, the very fire and passion and zeal of God, that takes a hold of our spirits, to take us beyond the comfort zone of the natural world we live in.

Thank you for Your commission, O God, that You entrust Your saints, Your sons with, today, even in this book, You entrust us all with such a high calling, with such an honor to be Your ministers, Your representatives, Your ambassadors.

And together with Paul we would say today, Father, whatever gain we have, whatever ambition, whatever motivation, *if it does not line up with Yours we don't want it!* If it does not line up with the excellence of the knowledge of our redemption in Him, if it does not line up with the excellence of the knowledge of Jesus, if it does not line up with the excellence of the knowledge of the true gospel of God, *we count it as refuse,* Father.

We are not anxious about our next meal Father, because we already ate Your meat.

Thank you Father! Thank you Jesus!

Amen.

In closing, I urge you to get yourself a copy of *The Mirror Study Bible.* It is the best paraphrased translation of the Scriptures from the original Greek that I have ever read, because it reveals the nuances of God's heart and Paul's gospel the clearest. It's available online at Barnes & Noble and several other book sellers.

If you want me or someone from of our team to come to where you are, *anywhere in the world,* and give a talk, or teach you and some of your friends *about the gospel message and these redemption realities,* simply contact us at www.LivingWordIntl.com, or you can always find me on Facebook.

If your life has changed as a result of reading this book, *please write to me and let me know.*

I would love to share in your joy *so that my joy in writing this book may be full!*

"If you knew the gift of God,
and who it is that is saying to you,
'Give me a drink,'
you would have asked Him,
and He would have given you
living water.'
The woman said to Him,
'Sir, the well is deep and you have
nothing to draw with,
where would you get this living
water from,
are you greater than our father
Jacob who gave us this well and
drank from it himself, him and
his sons and his cattle?'

"Jesus said to her,
'Everyone who drinks of this
water will thirst again,

...but whoever drinks of the water
that I shall give him will never
thirst;

...the water that I shall give him
will become in him a spring of
water welling up to eternal life."

-John 4:10-14

About the Author

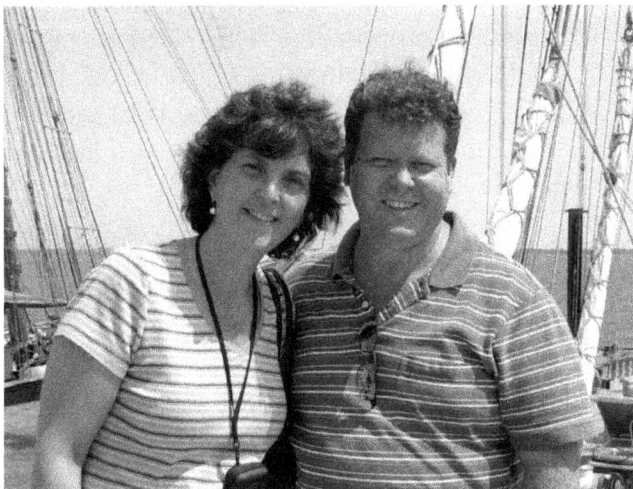

Rudi & Carmen Louw together oversee: Living Word International.

They also travel and minister both locally and internationally.

Rudi was born and raised in the country of South Africa, while Carmen grew up in Cortland, New York.

They function in the ministry of reconciliation (2 Corinthians 5:18-21) and flow strongly with the Holy Spirit and His anointing to teach, preach, prophesy, heal, and whatever is needed to touch people's lives with the reality of God's love and power.

God has given them keen insight into what He has to say to mankind in the work of redemption concerning the revelation and restoration of humanity's true identity.

Therefore they emphasize THE GOSPEL, IN CHRIST REALITIES, the GRACE of God, the WORD OF RIGHTEOUSNESS, *and all such eternal truths essential to salvation and living the CHRIST-LIFE.*

They have been granted this wisdom and revelation into the knowledge of God by the Spirit of Truth; that resurrected Spirit of Jesus Christ, *to establish and strengthen believers in the faith of God, and to activate them in ministering to others.*

Not only are people set free from the poison and bondage of sin, condemnation and all kinds of intimidation, (upheld, strengthened and reinforced by age old religious ideas born out of ignorance) **but many are brought into a closer more intimate relationship with Father God, as Daddy**, through accurate teaching and unveiling of the gospel message, prophetic words, healings and miracles.

Rudi & Carmen are closely knitted together with many other effective Christians, church fellowships, and groups of believers who share the same revelation and passion *to impart the truth of the gospel to others, and so* **to impact and transform the world we live in with the LOVE and POWER of God.**